Praise For

# POETRY WILL SAVE YOUR LIFE

"This book will open worlds."
—Will Schwalbe, bestselling author of
*The End of Your Life Book Club*

"Every passage feels like a private gift."
— Hope Jahren, bestselling author of *Lab Girl*

"The intersection of art and life has rarely been so vividly rendered."
—Daphne Merkin, author of *This Close to Happy*

"Charming and captivating."
—Andrew Solomon, author of *Far From the Tree*

"Empathic, wise, humane, and consoling."
—Meghan O'Rourke, author of *The Long Goodbye*

"Bialosky writes with a sincerity that would have made Dickinson herself weep."
—Mary-Louise Parker, author of *Dear Mr. You*

"An emotional, sometimes-wrenching account of how lines of poetry can be lifelines."
–*Kirkus Reviews*

"Candid and canny . . . Bialosky's erudite and instructive approach to poetry [is] itself a refreshing tonic."

*—Chicago Tribune*


"A lovely hybrid that blends [Bialosky's] coming-of-age story with engaging literary analysis . . . [It] demonstrates how poems can become an integral part of life. It also suggests, on every page, the wisdom and deep compassion that make [Bialosky's book] a tremendous asset both to readers and other writers."

*—The Washington Post*


"An intimate rendering of a poet's passion for words."

*—Publishers Weekly* (Starred Review)


"Bialosky's attention to detail and love of language serve the reader well. This is a book to savor."

*—Library Journal*


"An intimate discussion not only on how to *read* poetry, but also on how to *love* poetry . . . Bialosky convinces us that poetry is alive and ready to breathe with us—through love, loss, joy, pain, and the immensity of experience life brings us."

*—Christian Science Monitor*


"Unusual and affecting . . . This lovely memoir poignantly and credibly shows how [poetry] can inspire our acceptance of life."

—Hilma Wolitzer, *East Hampton Star*

**ATRIA**
PAPERBACK

An Imprint of Simon & Schuster, Inc.
1230 Avenue of the Americas
New York, NY 10020

First Atria Paperback edition October 2018

**ATRIA** PAPERBACK and colophon are trademarks
of Simon & Schuster, Inc.

For information about special discounts for bulk purchases,
please contact Simon & Schuster Special Sales at 1-866-506-1949
or business@simonandschuster.com.

The Simon & Schuster Speakers Bureau can bring authors
to your live event. For more information or to book an event,
contact the Simon & Schuster Speakers Bureau at 1-866-248-3049
or visit our website at www.simonspeakers.com.

Interior design by Michelle Marchese

Manufactured in the United States of America

10   9   8   7   6   5   4   3   2

Names: Bialosky, Jill, author.
Title: Poetry will save your life : a memoir / by Jill Bialosky.
Description: First Atria Books hardcover edition. | New York : Atria Books,
    2017. | Description based on print version record and CIP data provided by
    publisher; resource not viewed.
Identifiers: LCCN 2016056306 (print) | LCCN 2017015404 (ebook) | ISBN
    9781451693218 (eBook) | ISBN 9781451693201 (hardback)
Subjects: LCSH: Bialosky, Jill. | Poets, American--20th century--Biography. |
    American poetry--21st century. | BISAC: BIOGRAPHY & AUTOBIOGRAPHY /
    Personal Memoirs. | POETRY / Anthologies (multiple authors). | LITERARY
    COLLECTIONS / General.
Classification: LCC PS3552.I19 (ebook) | LCC PS3552.I19 Z46 2017 (print) |
    DDC 811/.54 [B] --dc23
LC record available at https://lccn.loc.gov/2016056306

ISBN 978-1-4516-9320-1
ISBN 978-1-9821-0482-5 (pbk)
ISBN 978-1-4516-9321-8 (ebook)

# POETRY WILL SAVE YOUR LIFE

A Memoir

# JILL BIALOSKY

**ATRIA** PAPERBACK

*New York   London   Toronto   Sydney   New Delhi*

For my mother, Iris Yvonne Bialosky

What is poetry which does not save
Nations or people?

—from "Dedication" by Czesław Miłosz

# CONTENTS

# PREFACE

I fell in love with poetry when my fourth grade teacher, Miss
Hudson, read us Robert Frost's "The Road Not Taken." I've
memorized that poem, and often, when I'm at a crossroads—
both literally and metaphorically—the lines come to me.
Since then, other poems have become guideposts. When it be-
gins to snow, I think of Wallace Stevens and "The Snow
Man" and the line "one must have a mind of winter." I've said
that line frequently enough in my head that it has become a
part of me. When I'm slightly down or feeling overlooked, I
think of Emily Dickinson's "I'm Nobody" and smile at my
lapse into self-pity. When I'm perplexed by how someone has
behaved, I remember T. S. Eliot's "humankind cannot bear
very much reality." When I'm suffering a loss or heartbreak, I
think of Elizabeth Bishop's "The art of losing isn't hard to
master," and its sly irony makes me feel less alone.

Stand by a window at night on the middle floor of a
high-rise in an urban city and watch the lights go on and off
in the apartment buildings across the street. Each building
contains a set of mini compartments, and in each compart-
ment resides a person . . . or perhaps a man and a woman, or
college roommates. A family with young children. Or an el-

derly person and her aide. A pair of lovers. Some of the windows are easier to see through and others are more opaque. In each small compartment, people tend to their daily rituals. They make love, drink, eat, and sleep. Curled into the cushions on a couch, they cry from bereavement or a broken heart. Or out of loneliness. Sometimes, on a hot day when the windows are open, you can hear strangers arguing or laughing. In these rooms, babies are conceived; people get sick and even die; someone might take his own life. Imagine in each of these small spaces, poems are taking shape, poems written from the experiences that occur inside and outside those rooms. Experiences that are both common and unique and a part of everyday living. Poems are made from the lives lived, borne out of experiences and shaped by solitary thought. Like a map to an unknown city, a poem might lead you toward an otherwise unreachable experience; but once you've reached it, you recognize it immediately.

For years I've flagged poems in individual volumes or anthologies with paper clips and Post-its. I have xeroxed poems and stuck them on my refrigerator or on bulletin boards. I have collected poems as someone else might collect stamps or coins or works of art—amazed by the many human experiences, large and small, that find their meeting place in poems. Poetry has given me more sustenance, meaning, joy, and consolation than I could hope for in this life, and in return, it is my hope that this book might open the door to poetry for others. My method is to offer some of the poems that found me along certain crucial moments in my coming of age, or poems that later brought back a particular memory or experience to locate the ways in which poems document

the mental and emotional, conscious and unconscious pro-
cesses that lie underneath the everyday actions of men and
women.

Poems are composed of our own language disordered, re-
configured, reimagined, and compressed in ways that offer a
heightened sense of reality and embrace a common human-
ity. A poem, in fact, possesses a consciousness, the conscious-
ness of the maker, and I have found that in that sense, a poem
in its condensed form casts its own light on the ways in which
we live in the world.

How did I fall in love with poetry? As a young girl living
in the wake of my father's early death, I was desperate for
tenderness and love. Poems were a source of comfort, once I
discovered them. I was aware that another person had spent
time writing them, and I felt that they were an act of gener-
osity and devotion to other human beings, to other readers. I
found love and tenderness in certain poems, in others cruelty
and brutality—no matter what they took as their subjects.
And I felt, in a strange way, that poetry saved me from the
less interesting, emptier life I'd have lived had I not discov-
ered it.

Poems are a form of mythmaking, as they seek to create a
unified vision of cosmic, social, and primal life order. Because
of their compact and compressed form, they are immediate
and intimate. A poem enters the reader or listener, inhabits
her, so that its meaning is, in a sense, superfluous to the expe-
rience of encountering it. This memoir is also a form of
mythmaking, for experiences are heightened, altered, and
shaped by the form in which they are told. *Poetry Will Save
Your Life* is not a full telling of a life, nor can a memoir ever

be such. Oxford describes a memoir as "a historical account or biography written from personal knowledge or special sources." My sources are poems, and the poems I present provide—to a certain extent—a window into my way of thinking and associating. Such is the mystery and wonder of a poem. This book might have collected a hundred poems, or a thousand poems. The possibilities are infinite. Like viewing an album of photographs, I can chart my history by the poems I've chosen to write about, remembering exactly when and where I first came upon it and what it meant to me then and means to me now.

But I have also shaped this book with the clear awareness that a poem doesn't just have one life or one influence on a single life—like mine—however lasting. It also has an afterlife. That after-existence in the memory of the reader can be intellectually, analytically, even technically focused, while still preserving the integrity and wonder of the first encounter. And so I have organized this book to try to suggest both existences in my mind and my memory because, in the end, both are necessary to honor the art.

# DISCOVERY

## THE ROAD NOT TAKEN
Robert Frost

I am a child sitting in my wooden flip-top desk in my fourth grade classroom listening to Miss Hudson read Robert Frost's poem "The Road Not Taken," a poem about two paths and a crossroad. Miss Hudson is in love with literature. She reads aloud to the class, gesturing madly with her arms as she recites the verse, revealing the sweat rings on her dress underneath her armpits, saliva forming in the corner of her mouth. I look at my classmates sitting in identical desks, the sunlight showing the ink stains, carved initials, and cracks in the wood. One girl is tall and big with a beautiful face and curly white hair. Another has skinny legs and wears knee-high socks. Another girl is the class bombshell. The boy in the back row has a "Vote for Kennedy" button pinned on his peacoat. I imagine my classmates lead perfect lives with perfect families. Are they equally mesmerized? My face is round and my hair is cut short around my face, bangs held back with a bobby pin. I am an awkward, uncomfortable child, ill at ease among others. The humiliations are growing: I'm embarrassed at how ridiculous I look in the short, blue, one-piece gym suit. I worry I'll stumble in my attempt to straddle the horse in gym class, or that I'll be picked last for Capture the Flag. I am embarrassed by the agonizing weigh-ins. In music class I dread having to sing scales aloud and hitting the wrong note. I can barely keep my chin up or will myself not to blush when I'm called on. And then Miss Hudson reads us this poem and I'm transfixed.

## THE ROAD NOT TAKEN
### Robert Frost (1874–1963)

Two roads diverged in a yellow wood,
And sorry I could not travel both
And be one traveler, long I stood
And looked down one as far as I could
To where it bent in the undergrowth;

Then took the other, as just as fair,
And having perhaps the better claim,
Because it was grassy and wanted wear;
Though as for that the passing there
Had worn them really about the same,

And both that morning equally lay
In leaves no step had trodden black.
Oh, I kept the first for another day!
Yet knowing how way leads on to way,
I doubted if I should ever come back.

I shall be telling this with a sigh
Somewhere ages and ages hence:
Two roads diverged in a wood, and I—
I took the one less traveled by,
And that has made all the difference.

My father died when I was two. He suffered a heart attack while bowling in a couples' league at the local alley. Once, I thought it was playing basketball. The stories morph into their own memory and shape. I imagine him thrusting the bowling ball up against his chest, cradling it, letting it go, the ball spinning down the aisle, knocking down all the pins, and then, in an instant, all the lights go out. I cannot imagine any further. At night, I lie in my bed and think about my father, as if to will him into memory from the pictures my mother keeps in a photo album. When I look at his face in the photos I try to find mine in it. Do I have his eyes, his mouth, his intellect? I know I don't possess his athletic prowess. My mother is a young widow with three children under the age of three. There is no language in my home or my sheltered suburban world to help me understand why that one event marked my life.

As a young girl, I read my own story in "The Road Not Taken." There are two roads one might travel: The road where families are whole and not broken, and fathers don't die young, and mothers are happy—where everything seems to fit together like pieces in a puzzle; and the road I travel, which is crooked and not quite right, with bumps along the way. I know it is important I choose the right course. I struggle in math and science. Reading books has already trumped all else, and through Frost I discover a language where words are organized to convey feeling and meaning. The clear voice of the poet comes through the mouth of Miss Hudson. The voice is intimate and commanding and through the verse's descriptive powers, I read my own experience in its narrative. In essence, I intuit the poet in solitary thought and take to the richness and layers of meaning hunkered in the words.

My father's early death separates me from my peers who I presume have not experienced an early loss, who have not borne witness to sorrow in a house—a mother grieving, a world torn apart by tragedy. Though of course they too must have suffered their own private losses and tragedies. A child always thinks she is alone in her sorrow. In our small circle of family and friends, we are known as my mother's poor daughters. Tragedy makes us self-conscious. When we enter a room people stare. I wonder if our faces are somehow marked by our father's death in a way I can't see. If only someone would talk about what's happened to us, but fear keeps conversation at bay. Tragedy is a hush-hush topic, something nice people don't discuss.

When Miss Hudson recites "The Road Not Taken," I form a picture in my mind of two roads diverging. One road is worn and tended and it is evident it is the road most traveled. The other—overgrown, shaded, and magical—calls out to me. If I travel it, what life might I discover? There's more than one way and suddenly I'm included. I belong.

———

Reading the Frost poem as an adult, I experience its meaning differently. Frost might have intended for the tone of the last stanza to be ironic ("I shall be telling this with a sigh"). Perhaps the implication is that the two roads were in actuality "really about the same," that they "equally lay / In leaves no step had trodden black," and that choosing one rather than the other was an impulsive, casual decision made simply because the road taken had "perhaps the better claim."

I attend a lecture where a poet references "The Road Not Taken." He reads it as a poem about depression and mental illness, and in the lines "leaves no step had trodden black" and the doubtful "if I should ever come back," he infers the fear that Frost, or the poem's speaker, might never emerge from his depressive state. And Frost can be darkly droll. An undercurrent runs through his seemingly wholesome verse, and juxtaposing the dark undercurrent with accessible, everyday language gives his work potency. In "Death of the Hired Man" he writes, "Home is the place where, when you have to go there, / They have to take you in."

A poem's meaning alters by the associations, insights, and experience we bring to it. We may respond to the poem for meaning, or because we fall under the spell of its musicality and end rhymes, or because we are drawn to the poem's sense of irony and wit, or its visual imagery. A poem can do many things at once. Like "The Road Not Taken," it can challenge the reader intellectually, spiritually, and emotionally. It can validate our experiences or cause us to question our beliefs. Robert Frost wrote that "poetry is when an emotion has found its thought and the thought has found words."

# DANGER

**WE REAL COOL**
Gwendolyn Brooks
**RICHARD CORY**
Edwin Arlington Robinson

One day, a new girl moves into the house behind mine. I'll call her Marie. She has blond hair and dark-brown, sensitive eyes. She hears me in the backyard bouncing my rubber ball against the tarred pavement of our driveway and wanders over. We become best friends. Every day after school, she comes to my house or I go to hers. In the summer we draw hopscotch boards on the pavement with chalk or jump rope to playground jingles. "Miss Mary Mack" is our favorite. In the winter we huddle in her bedroom or mine and play with our Barbie dolls, imitating the seductive world of adults. Sometimes we go into the clubhouse behind her house and show each other our flat chests wondering when we'll get bumps.

Years before, her mother suffered a stroke and became paralyzed on one side of her body and ever since has been in a wheelchair. When I go over to Marie's house, her mother greets us warmly and with her one useful arm prepares peanut butter sandwiches and glasses of cold milk for us in the kitchen. It is as if she has waited all day for her daughter to come home and she wheels her chair up to the table and sits with us while we eat our sandwiches. We tell her about our day at school while their rambunctious dog yaps at our heels. Her father is rarely home.

We are in sixth grade when the curtain of our innocence drops. Marie's mother dies suddenly. Before we have a chance to process the loss, her father remarries (how can this happen so fast—yet it does) and they move miles away to another suburb, forty-five minutes from mine. One day Marie calls and invites me for a sleepover. I haven't seen her in over a year, an interval in which both of us have grown from young girls to adolescents. My mother pulls up on the driveway of Marie's new house to drop me off, and I have butterflies in my stomach. Marie runs out of the house to greet me. In the year since I have seen her, she has grown beautiful, and her face has taken on complexity. Her hair is long down her back and she wears a peasant blouse, blue jean cut-offs, and hippie lace-up sandals. To me, who is uncomfortable with her own body, she seems the most perfect being, her golden skin glowing in the hot sun, and I am enchanted by her all over again. She grabs my hand and within minutes it is as if no time has passed.

Her father and stepmother are out for dinner, and we have the entire house to ourselves. She doesn't like her stepmother. She puts her finger in her mouth and makes gagging noises. She asks if I want a cigarette, opens a drawer in the kitchen, takes out a pack of her stepmother's Virginia Slims from the carton there, and lights one. I have never smoked a cigarette. Just as we're getting settled, three boys from her new town come over. We trail down to the basement—turned into a playroom—and listen to music. One of the boys has brought a bottle of tequila. We do a shot or two and quickly the room falls out of kilter. The three boys stare at Marie with open lust and I can't blame them. She is magnificent. I look down at myself and see that I haven't quite developed yet. My hair has thankfully grown out and is long and wavy, but it can't hide my flat chest. Will I always look like this?

Eventually, one boy takes Marie's hand and brings her to the laundry room off the playroom to make out. It seems like forever that she's gone. I awkwardly try to make conversation with the two other boys, who I know each wish they had taken Marie's hand. To my relief, Marie's father and stepmother come home, and her tall, military-like father, whom I studied when we were children, fascinated by fathers, commands the boys to leave. We go upstairs to Marie's new bedroom and talk late into the night, analyzing aspects of each of the three boys until we fall asleep.

When my mother comes to pick me up the next morning and I say goodbye to Marie, I am consumed by dread and worry. I don't want to leave her alone in that big, cold, airy house. Over time, because of the long distance between our neighborhoods, we grow apart and eventually lose touch. I hear that she hangs out with a wild crowd who smoke pot and take drugs, and the thought fills me with a strange emotion I have no name for. I feel excluded and protective at the same time. I can't imagine how her father will tolerate this behavior. More years pass. Then one terrible day, when I am in my late teens, we learn she has shot herself in the head with a pistol her father kept hidden in the house. Her funeral is the darkest day I can remember. How did this happen? I am frightened by all I know and don't know.

## WE REAL COOL

Gwendolyn Brooks (1917–2000)

The Pool Players.
Seven at the Golden Shovel.

We real cool. We
Left school. We

Lurk late. We
Strike straight. We

Sing sin. We
Thin gin. We

Jazz June. We
Die soon.

———

Many years later, when I come across this searing poem by Gwendolyn Brooks with its nod to the rhythm of the streets, I am struck by how it turns the familiar playground jingle on its head. Suddenly I'm brought back to the memory of jumping rope with Marie to "Miss Mary Mack," with little knowledge of all the perils and vulnerability that growing up held. Though the poem isn't directly about suicide, the last line evokes its dark hue.

Gwendolyn Brooks, the first black poet to win the Pulitzer Prize, grew up in Chicago, and her poems document the everyday lives of black Chicagoans. Of Brooks's poems, the poet Sonia Sanchez writes, "Each time I revisit her poems, they climb up on my knees and sit in tight contentment. They speak to me of form and color, patterns and dawns. They talk of myths; they tell me where the flesh lives. . . ." The poem uses vernacular language to show us the dangers of being "cool." Rhyme, rhythm, syntax and repetition achieve memorability. A poem's music and rhythm can become embedded in our consciousness like a haunting jazz tune or a schoolyard chant. The use of irony—we real cool, we left school—sears the poem into our minds. The poem gives us a warning. It calls attention to that thin line between "being cool," and the slide into darkness and danger. It asks what is in us that turns away from the dance? It both lulls and disturbs; a cautionary tale of what can happen when we cross over the line. "We Real Cool" should be taped on the refrigerator of every house with a teenager.

## RICHARD CORY

### Edwin Arlington Robinson (1869–1935)

Whenever Richard Cory went down town,
We people on the pavement looked at him:
He was a gentleman from sole to crown,
Clean favored, and imperially slim.

And he was always quietly arrayed,
And he was always human when he talked;

But still he fluttered pulses when he said,
"Good-morning," and he glittered when he walked.

And he was rich—yes, richer than a king—
And admirably schooled in every grace:
In fine, we thought that he was everything
To make us wish that we were in his place.

So on we worked, and waited for the light,
And went without the meat, and cursed the bread;
And Richard Cory, one calm summer night,
Went home and put a bullet through his head.

This ballad describes a wealthy, educated gentleman who is admired by his community. Walking through town, dressed in fine clothes, no one suspects that he will take his own life. Though it is about a man and written during the Great Depression, a time when people survived on day-old bread, anyone past or present who has been blindsided by a suicide can connect with it. Richard Cory becomes a stand-in for every man and woman. Reading it, I'm reminded of how deceptive outer appearances can be. Just as I never imagined that beneath Marie's lovely veneer she suffered so deeply, and at one particular cataclysmic moment, a confluence of forces came together and life proved untenable. It is no wonder the poem endures nearly a century after it first appeared, adapted into a song by Paul Simon, and that its maker, Edwin Arlington Robinson—himself a quiet, introverted, reclusive man—was considered one of the greatest poets in America at the time of his death.

# WONDER

## THE STAR
Jane Taylor and Ann Taylor

We're driving in our gray sedan in the dark. I am in the passenger seat next to my mother, my bare thighs, in shorts, sticking to the fake leather. Whenever the car comes to a sudden halt, her hand flies out to protect me from going into the windshield. It is a coveted spot. As one of three girl siblings, we fight fiercely to obtain it. It's late—way past our bedtime—and the sky is filled with hundreds of stars. It is moments like this, in the car with my mother, where my worries about our well-being usually vanish.

But on this night we are searching for Poggy, our black, frisky miniature poodle, who ran out of the house early that morning and has still not come home. He was a present from one of my mother's dates, a football player for the Cleveland Browns. My mother looks into the rearview mirror every now and then to check on my two sisters in the backseat. Tears are bubbling in my younger sister's eyes. The eldest is pressed against her window, twirling a strand of her long hair with her finger. I look back at my mother and then out my own window, which is filled with swirls of stars. I begin to recite the nursery rhyme "Twinkle, Twinkle, Little Star" in my head, a trick I've learned to help me keep calm. Later I will discover that the well-known verses from the nursery rhyme evolved from this poem.

## THE STAR

Jane Taylor (1783–1824)
and Ann Taylor (1782–1866)

Twinkle, twinkle, little star,
How I wonder what you are!
Up above the world so high,
Like a diamond in the sky.

When the blazing sun is gone,
When he nothing shines upon,
Then you show your little light,
Twinkle, twinkle, all the night.

Then the trav'ller in the dark
Thanks you for your tiny spark,
He could not see which way to go,
If you did not twinkle so.

In the dark blue sky you keep,
Often thro' my curtains peep,
For you never shut your eye,
Till the sun is in the sky.

'Tis your bright and tiny spark
Lights the trav'ller in the dark:
Tho' I know not what you are,
Twinkle, twinkle, little star.

At night, when I can't sleep, I go downstairs into the little hallway where Poggy sleeps and cuddle with him. I like the touch of the little rubbery pads on his feet and the beating of his restless heart. In the mornings, he scratches at the door, anxious for one of us to come and take him for a walk. Sometimes, locked in some kind of white heat, he scurries around our living room, dashing in and out of rooms as if he's suddenly lost his mind, which sends us girls into wails of laughter. What if we never find him?

We drive through the streets of our neighborhood for what seems like hours until we finally resign ourselves and go home. The next day, we go to the local kennel and call the Animal Protective League. Nothing. Days pass. At night, after the news, we watch a short program where lost dogs—beagles, golden retrievers, the occasional collie—appear on the screen, hoping we might see our black poodle. We never find him. I pray that he didn't get run over and found a better home for himself, but I'm puzzled all the same. Every day, I rush home from school hoping he's returned until, gradually, I learn to accept that he's not coming back.

———

*Twinkle, twinkle, little star, / How I wonder what you are.* A child looks up at the sky and sees a star as the personification of a being and wonders not so much what it is but, "what *you* are." The twinkling star comes to represent the miracle and mystery of the universe. The use of rhyme and repeated verse give the poem its childlike simplicity. The words sky, star, wonder, and diamond form a constellation of possibilities. A poem can open a window into the wonder and mystery of the galaxy and coax a child away from fear.

# SELFHOOD

## MY SHADOW and THE SWING
### Robert Louis Stevenson

Books are my secret companions. I sit in my bedroom and turn the pages of *The Lonely Doll*, a book about a girl named Edith who has no one to play with but her doll. I read *Little House on the Prairie*, *The Red Pony*, *The Red Badge of Courage*, and *The Yearling*. I like reading the poems from *A Child's Garden of Verse*. Sometimes I read them over without really knowing what they mean, simply liking the way the words sound. But when I leave my secret menagerie and am forced outside the comforts of my home, I don't quite know who I am or where I belong. After my father dies, we three sisters do everything together, while mom's still sleeping off a late night, or just not wanting to get up quite yet and face another day without her darling husband whose diamond ring she still wears on her finger, though she is wed now to the grave. We slip Pop-Tarts into the toaster for breakfast and later build card castles on the living room floor. We're always together. It's like we're one person, as if we're literally stitched together at the hip. While I'm shy and reserved, sister number three—the youngest—is fearless. She's not afraid to climb trees and explore the scary field at the end of our block. Though it is only a plot of abandoned land, it feels like a forest. Together, we get into mischief. Once we decide to run away from home, packing a jar of peanut butter and a sleeve of Saltines and hiding behind our house for an entire afternoon.

I am scared of birds, and on the way to school if a flock lands on the sidewalk in front of us, she shoos them away before we pass. Later, this fearless girl will go on to work on a landscape crew pulling out weeds and pushing mowers, nail a job pumping gas at our corner Sohio station, and ride a motorbike. But as a child she's disorganized and unable to sit still. My mother used to say she'd have to sit on her to change her diaper. Once, her teacher came into my classroom at the end of school and asked if I would help sister number three clean out her desk. Both of us were mortified.

Sister number one is the beauty, with long dark hair in braids and clear, fragile blue eyes. She has this way about her that makes her hard to refuse. At night, when my mother goes out, she convinces us to watch horror movies with her. My dreams become nightmares.

Every night I fall asleep to my sisters' sleep breathing in the beds across from mine. Though I feel as if I inhabit their being, as if they are *me*, sometimes I long to break free of them. I notice that on our way to school, our shadows on the pavement intertwine as we walk. I study them. If I walk ahead my shadow is my own. The meaning behind a poem I know by heart comes to life.

## MY SHADOW

### Robert Louis Stevenson (1850–1894)

I have a little shadow that goes in and out with me,
And what can be the use of him is more than I can see.
He is very, very like me from the heels up to the head;
And I see him jump before me, when I jump into my bed.

The funniest thing about him is the way he likes to grow—
Not at all like proper children, which is always very slow;
For he sometimes shoots up taller like an India-rubber ball,
And he sometimes gets so little that there's none of
    him at all.

He hasn't got a notion of how children ought to play,
And can only make a fool of me in every sort of way.
He stays so close beside me, he's a coward you can see;
I'd think shame to stick to nursie as that shadow
    sticks to me!

One morning, very early, before the sun was up,
I rose and found the shining dew on every buttercup;
But my lazy little shadow, like an arrant sleepy-head,
Had stayed at home behind me and was fast asleep in bed.

———

"My Shadow" celebrates a child's world of independence and
her own uniqueness. It is easy to memorize and perhaps that

is why this poem is often the first a child learns. When the speaker of the poem jumps into his bed, he can see his shadow on the wall jump in bed next to him. His shadow provides comfort and companionship. He owns it completely. The child finds pleasure in mocking his shadow for being lazy and not knowing how to play, and the mocking gives him power. While the poem shows the changing nature of a shadow on a wall, it also reveals the transformation of a child discovering his own power and individuality.

Summer days we spend exploring the circumference of our backyard and our block. We dig for worms and poke ants between the cracks in the driveway with twigs. We play kick-the-can in the street with other neighborhood kids. We draw hopscotch boards on the sidewalk with chalk. We jump rope. One day a truck pulls up the driveway and the driver unloads a red swing set with three swings, a seesaw, and a slide, a gift from another of my mother's boyfriends, and installs it in our backyard. We compete in swinging contests to see who can soar the highest. We swing until our stomachs are queasy, until the poles anchoring the set are pulled like roots from the earth, and we feel cherry bumps. Gradually one sister abandons her swing and goes inside, then the other trails behind her, and suddenly I am alone. I move myself back as far as I can go with the tips of my toes to the ground and then release my feet and begin to pump. I feel the wind in my hair, the smell of the summer flowers in the breeze. I close my eyes and soar over the roof of my

house, so that I can see into the wide girth of our neighbor-
hood. The world outside the small circumference of my
home and my family is in sight. Reachable. Maybe one day I
will soar beyond my own horizons.

## THE SWING
### Robert Louis Stevenson

How do you like to go up in a swing,
Up in the air so blue?
Oh, I do think it the pleasantest thing
Ever a child can do!

Up in the air and over the wall,
Till I can see so wide,
Rivers and trees and cattle and all
Over the countryside—

Till I look down on the garden green,
Down on the roof so brown—
Up in the air I go flying again,
Up in the air and down!

———

Robert Louis Stevenson was born in Edinburgh, Scotland on
November 13, 1850. He was a sickly child and reading Shake-
speare and *The Arabian Nights* kept him company in the many
long periods when he was at home convalescing. Perhaps it

was from those stories that his love of literature began. I wonder if the inspiration for "The Swing" began there—Stevenson sick and alone in his bed, feeling his own separateness. The poem's simple rhyme scheme and singsong cadence, which mimics the act of swinging, is cunningly deceptive. Embodied within the poem is the realization that as high as one soars, one must come down as well. Down to oneself. And looking down is scary. The poet Elizabeth Bishop in her autobiographical story, "The Country Mouse," writes about the realization of her own separateness on a visit with her aunt to the dentist's office. She sat outside reading *National Geographic*. This incident would evolve into her splendid poem "In the Waiting Room." In her story she writes: "A feeling of absolute and utter desolation came over me. I felt . . . myself. In a few days it would be my seventh birthday. I felt I, I, I, and looked at the three strangers in panic. I was one of them too, inside my scabby body and wheezing lungs."

"The Swing" recalls that same frightful realization of one's own solitary self, sailing over the lip of the horizon "up in the air and down."

# MEMORY

## I WANDERED LONELY AS A CLOUD
William Wordsworth

My son is away at college, my husband is working, and I'm
on my own, out for a walk on Gibson beach, in a pensive,
solitary mood. It's December, white clouds billow in the
blue sky, it's fifty degrees, and there is not another person
in sight. I walk, stopping to pick up a seashell or a white
stone that catches my eye. I turn back toward where I came
from and notice the trail of my own footsteps imprinted in
the sand. Slowly the brightness of the sun dancing on the
water begins to lift me out of my melancholy state. I re-
member walking this same stretch of beach with my son
fifteen years ago when he was a boy of maybe five or six.
He held my hips and followed in my footsteps and we
chanted, *chug-a-chuga chug-a-chuga, choo, choo,* forming a
mini train in the hot sand. Alone on the beach, I feel the
essence of my son in the salty breeze. I remember the way
the sun reflected off his shiny blond hair, his fair skin
slathered with sunblock, his sunny disposition. The mem-

ory lifts my spirits, and when I return home I think about it again, in much the same way William Wordsworth reflected upon his earlier encounter with the daffodils in this lovely poem.

## I WANDERED LONELY AS A CLOUD
### William Wordsworth (1770–1850)

I wandered lonely as a cloud
That floats on high o'er vales and hills,
When all at once I saw a crowd,
A host, of golden daffodils;
Beside the lake, beneath the trees,
Fluttering and dancing in the breeze.

Continuous as the stars that shine
And twinkle on the milky way,
They stretched in never-ending line
Along the margin of a bay:
Ten thousand saw I at a glance,
Tossing their heads in sprightly dance.

The waves beside them danced; but they
Out-did the sparkling waves in glee:
A poet could not but be gay,
In such a jocund company:
I gazed—and gazed—but little thought
What wealth the show to me had brought:

For oft, when on my couch I lie
In vacant or in pensive mood,
They flash upon that inward eye
Which is the bliss of solitude;
And then my heart with pleasure fills,
And dances with the daffodils.

———

Robert Louis Stevenson's "The Swing," published in 1913 in *A Child's Garden of Verse*, may have been inspired by this William Wordsworth poem written between 1804–1807. The two poems share a similar cadence and celebrate the surprise of the natural world. The poem was inspired by William Wordsworth and his sister Dorothy Wordsworth's visit to Glencoyne Park on April 15, 1802. Dorothy Wordsworth describes the encounter in her journal:

> When we were in the woods beyond Gowbarrow Park, we saw a few daffodils close to the water side. We fancied that the lake had floated the seed ashore & that the little colony had so sprung up—but as we went along there were more & more & at last under the boughs of the trees, we saw that there was a long belt of them along the shore, about the breadth of a country turnpike road. I never saw daffodils so beautiful they grew among the mossy stones about & about them, some rested their heads upon these stones as on a pillow for weariness & the rest tossed & reeled & danced & seemed as if they verily laughed with

the wind that blew upon them over the lake, they looked
so gay ever dancing ever changing.

"I Wander Lonely as a Cloud" tells a story of the poet, lone-
some from a day of solitary work, who wanders into a field
beside a lake and is greeted by a "host" of "golden daffodils"
dancing in the breeze. There are "ten thousand" of them,
tossing "their heads in sprightly dance." The sight fills him
with amusement and pleasure. It remains in his memory.
When the poet is pensive and his "inward eye" recalls the
daffodils, the memory fills his solitude with pleasure.

In his *Preface to Lyrical Ballads*, Wordsworth famously
described the poetic process this way: "I have said that poetry
is the spontaneous overflow of powerful feelings; it takes its
origin from emotion recollected in tranquility." Surely "I
Wandered Lonely as a Cloud" reads as an example of that be-
lief. Though the poem opens in a melancholic mood, it is a
happy poem, perhaps simply because the sight of daffodils
after a long winter is uplifting. It celebrates the comfort of
reexperiencing those things that delight or soothe us. Every
spring, when daffodils shoot up in the malls on Park Avenue
or in Central Park, I think of this poem, an ode to a flower
and to memory, and bask in their yellow glow.

# SHAME

## YOU AND YOUR WHOLE RACE
and I, TOO
Langston Hughes

The yellow school bus picks us up in the driveway of our school, snug in a pristine suburb where houses—each on its own small square of land—are surrounded by freshly mani-cured lawns and sprawling maple and oak trees. We are on our way to a field trip downtown to see the Terminal Tower and then to the art museum. Or maybe these were two differ-ent field trips, converged and conflated in my mind to mark the moment when the world and its injustices beyond my own small circumference lodged themselves in my psyche.

As we leave the suburbs, squished side by side in our seats, the bus takes us through the rundown sections of Cleveland known as the ghetto. It's late October, and from the school bus window, black children dressed in thin, torn coats, with no stockings, are playing on a porch. Why aren't they in school? A group of men are huddled together on a street corner passing a bottle in a paper bag. The bus drives past homes of pastel colors where the paint is chipped and porches sag to the ground. On some houses, newspaper is taped to the windows to block out the impending cold. Slowly the ghetto recedes, and we move into the industrial section of Cleveland, where smoke from factories leaves a trail of black smog in the sky, and then toward a cluster of tall steel buildings in Public Square. The bus stops and our teacher points out the tallest building in Cleveland, called the Terminal Tower, a name that scares me. Inside is the train terminal, the last stop on the rapid transit, conceived so that passengers from the suburbs would have a swift commute to work downtown. The tower houses hundreds of offices, where predominantly men and their secretaries go to work. I imagine these men and women inside their individual offices conducting business and then, at six o'clock, rushing out in a flood to catch the train. Suddenly, life outside my home and tiny world is illuminated in all its fascination and wonder. After craning our necks to view the tower, we get back on the bus and head to the museum. Soon the bus takes us up a long drive. We unload in single file at the museum entrance, hang our coats in the coatroom, and are given a little fold-up stool to carry with us while the guide escorts us through the rooms of the museum. I'm maybe ten or eleven. I think about the contrast of having traveled from the suburbs, through the city's ghetto where cars without tires sit on the side of the road, some houses vacant, then downtown where people work, and now to this modern building where we are told valuable artifacts from earlier civilizations are kept. Inside the pristine museum, so quiet you can hear our footsteps in our saddle shoes and loafers slap the marble floor, are valuable paintings, statues, pottery, and antiquities. It is as if each gallery—Asian, Egyptian, Medieval—opens a window into its own particular time and place. My mind is spinning. I can't seem to take it all in. We walk outside and stand in front of Rodin's *The Thinker*, a statue of a man in a thinking pose—his arm resting on his knee, chin cupped in his hand—a statue in honor of contemplation. But I'm still haunted by the image of the children on the stoop of one of the run-down houses, swinging on the porch rails, and wondering how they will survive the brutal winter with newspapers taped over their windows. I think of hundreds of men dressed in business suits carrying their briefcases to work and wonder why the men on the street corners in the ghetto don't have jobs too. Something isn't right.

We view many paintings that day: *Fight Between a Tiger and a Buffalo* by Henri Rousseau; Salvador Dalí's eerie and nightmarish *The Dream*; *The Crucifixion of St. Andrew* by Caravaggio—just as haunting as the Dalí painting. But it is the images of the ramshackle streets of East Cleveland that stay and haunt me. Back inside the bus, tired from traipsing through the airless, claustrophobic museum, we drive back home. I can't stop thinking about the ghetto, where smashed beer bottles, crushed soda cans, and fast-food wrappers litter the streets, as the bus leads us into our immaculate suburb. And as I look out the window at the rows of white painted houses with black shutters or brick colonials that line our streets, some with wreaths on the front door, I'm ashamed. Why us and not them? I'm suddenly afraid. My mother complains about all the bills stacking up and she worries about having enough money. I wonder if we'll end up one day in the ghetto. When I come across the poems by Langston Hughes, I remember my own sense of bewilderment and shame, and worse, my gratitude, for nothing more than the accident of being born into white privilege.

## YOU AND YOUR WHOLE RACE
Langston Hughes (1902–1967)

You and your whole race.
Look down upon the town in which you live
And be ashamed.
Look down upon white folks
And upon yourselves
And be ashamed
That such supine poverty exists there,
That such stupid ignorance breeds children there,
Behind such humble shelters of despair—
That you yourselves have not the sense to care
Nor the manhood to stand up and say
I dare you to come one step nearer, evil world,
With your hands of greed seeking to touch my
    throat, I dare you to come one step nearer me:
        When you can say that
        you will be free!


## I, TOO
Langston Hughes

I, too, sing America.

I am the darker brother.
They send me to eat in the kitchen
When company comes,

But I laugh,
And eat well,
And grow strong.

Tomorrow,
I'll be at the table
When company comes.
Nobody'll dare
Say to me,
"Eat in the kitchen,"
Then.

Besides,
They'll see how beautiful I am
And be ashamed—

I, too, am America.

———

Langston Hughes's poetry is known for its insightful depiction of black life in America. He was born in Joplin, Missouri. His parents divorced when he was a young child and afterward he was cared for primarily by his grandmother in Lawrence, Kansas. When his grandmother died in 1915, he moved to Lincoln, Illinois and then Cleveland, Ohio to live with his mother and her second husband. He attended high school in Cleveland. Enduring a childhood of loneliness and dislocation, he retreated into the "wonderful world of books." He published his first poems and stories in his high school magazine. When he was nineteen he wrote "The Negro Speaks of Rivers," the poem that launched his career after it was published in the *Crisis*, edited by W. E. B. Du Bois, about his deep heritage as seen through the rivers stemming back to the Euphrates and the Nile, to the "singing of the Mississippi when Abe Lincoln went to New Orleans." Paul Laurence Dunbar, Carl Sandburg, Claude McKay, and Walt Whitman were his poetic influences. In poems about and for African Americans, influenced by jazz and blues, he documented the experiences of urban figures such as elevator operators, cabaret singers, and streetwalkers. His famous poem about America, "I, Too," with echoes of Walt Whitman's "Song of Myself," calls for the inclusion of black voices not only in the poetic canon but also in America itself.

The poem is partially inspired by a trip Hughes took when he secured a job as a mess boy on a freighter bound for Africa. As the boat pulled out to sea he decided to throw all of his books into the ocean. "It was like throwing a million bricks out of my heart for it wasn't only the books I wanted to throw away, but everything unpleasant and miserable out of my past: the memory of my father, the poverties and uncertainty of my mother's life, the stupidities of color-prejudice, black in a white world . . . " The only book he did not throw overboard was Walt Whitman's *Leaves of Grass*.

Along with the poem "I, too," it is hard to recall Langston Hughes without thinking of his poem "Dreams," whose lines "Hold fast to dreams / For if dreams die / Life is a broken-winged bird / That cannot fly," become more potent and necessary if we read them alongside his poems that long for an America where the races live in equality.

Perhaps what makes these poems visceral is that the figures who reside within them come to life. In "I, Too," the boy, no doubt the son of a servant or slave, who is asked to retreat to the kitchen when company comes is made human. His pain and declaration of strength are telegraphed to the reader, allowing for an outpouring of our own manifestations of injustice and shame.

# ANCESTORS

## PSALM 23: "THE LORD IS MY SHEPHERD"

Poetry follows me to Hebrew school on Saturday mornings when the rabbi reads from the Song of Solomon and tells elaborate tales from the Bible. We learn the prayers for bread and wine, prayers for particular holidays, prayers to honor the dead. Many of them begin with these Hebrew words: *Baruch atah Adonai Eloheinu*. Blessed are you, Lord, our God, King of the universe.

At my grandmother's graveside on the morning of her funeral, the rabbi asks us to recite in unison the King James Version of Psalm 23, and our collective voices in the gray afternoon form a chorus of grief and mourning. After the prayer, we sprinkle a handful of soil onto her closed coffin. The casting of soil from the ground and the reciting of the psalm are rituals of mourning that allow us to honor the dead and seal the loved one in memory. As I recite the psalm along with the other mourners who have gathered at the gravesite, I think of my father in his dwelling place and his mother, my grandmother, now with him, and that one day I too will be dwelling in the house of the Lord forever. Does it matter whether heaven is a real physical place or a place of spirit? That the psalm may have been written as a myth of consolation? Aren't these collective hieroglyphs of faith the things that sustain us? Aren't poems the same as prayers?

My father's mother was from Vilna, Poland, a predominantly Jewish city on the border of Poland and Lithuania, before the Nazis invaded and it became a Nazi-run ghetto. She left the old country for America and married my grandfather when she was sixteen. Her sister stayed behind and did not survive the Holocaust. My grandmother's accent is thick and foreign, and in her strained pronunciations of English are echoes of pain and displacement.

On Friday nights, we sometimes celebrate Shabbat at their home. Every time my grandmother opens the door to greet us, her eyes well up. While I had lost a father and my mother a husband, my grandmother had lost her sister and her only son. She sees her son in us. As we sit around her dining room table, the room smelling of roasted brisket, I listen to their stories and watch my nearly silent grandfather, dressed in a white shirt, his pants held up by suspenders, pile his food on the back of his fork with his knife before putting it in his mouth, the way I learned they did in the old country. As I look at my grandparents, one at each end of the long table, I wonder what it was like for my father to grow up with them. Psalm 23 reminds me of the spirit of my ancestors, of those who came before me that I did not know, but whose essence live within me.

## PSALM 23: "THE LORD IS MY SHEPHERD"

The Lord is my shepherd; I shall not want.
He maketh me to lie down in green pastures: he
leadeth me beside the still waters.
He restoreth my soul: he leadeth me in the paths of
righteousness for his name's sake.
Yea, though I walk through the valley of the shadow
of death, I will fear no evil: for thou art with me;
thy rod and thy staff they comfort me.
Thou preparest a table before me in the presence of
mine enemies: thou anointest my head with oil;
my cup runneth over.
Surely goodness and mercy shall follow me all the
days of my life: and I will dwell in the house of
the Lord forever.

———

In Jewish tradition, Psalm 23 is recited traditionally at the mourner's Yizkor service, the service at the end of weekly service to mourn and bless those who have died. The book of Psalms is the backbone of the Hebrew prayer book, and Psalm 23 is the most famous. Jewish tradition attributes authorship of the book of Psalms to King David. Many of the psalms I have said so often, I can recite them by heart. The verse is a part of my inner vocabulary. When I go to synagogue and recite the psalm, my eyes fill with tears in remembrance.

The poet Jean Valentine says: "For me, there's a likeness between poetry and prayer that is not so much thanks or supplication or other conscious activity, but the more unconscious activity of meditation or dreaming. The likeness lies in poetry and meditative prayer and dreaming all being (potentially anyhow) healing, and all being out of our hands. For me, poetry is mostly silence. The deeper the better." What is it exactly about this psalm that is consoling? Is it our familiarity with it? Or the power of its words? Or its seeming innocence in the face of death?

## MY CHILD BLOSSOMS SADLY
Yehuda Amichai

Every Saturday morning, my mother loads us into the car, ignoring our groans, and drives us to Hebrew school. We hate it. We dislike the uninspired housewives disguised as teachers who embarrass us when we stumble over our Hebrew. Why does our Hebrew book begin at the end instead of at the beginning? Sometimes we cut class and hide in the girls' bathroom until the first hour of Hebrew school is over. The second hour is when we go into the auditorium for services and listen to the rabbi's sermon. Afterward, while we wait for our mother to pick us up, and remarkably she is always late, we steal little pastries from the Bar Mitzvah reception in the lobby. Though I hate Hebrew school with a passion, I love our rabbi. His skin is dark and tan, and he has a soft, guttural voice that reminds me of my grandfather from the old country. His stories come alive when he tells them. I can picture Joseph's vivid robe of many colors and the Red Sea parting. Every year he tells the story of Abraham and Isaac.

Sarah and Abraham have a son named Isaac. God wants to know if Abraham will obey him, so God tells him to sacrifice Isaac on a mountaintop. Abraham loves his son without question, but he also wants to obey God. He takes his son to the mountaintop. His son carries the wood and Abraham has brought a knife so that they can make an altar. Isaac asks where the lamb is that they will sacrifice. Abraham tells Isaac not to worry. He does as God instructed. He makes an altar and a fire and binds Isaac to prepare him for the sacrifice.

I grow frightened. Will Abraham kill his own son for God?

The rabbi pauses for effect, and an eerie silence fills the congregation. Then he begins again. An angel appears to Abraham and tells him not to sacrifice his son. He has obeyed God, and that is enough.

For days I think about this story. What does it mean? If I follow the Ten Commandments, will God favor me as well and save me from being the victim of terrible acts and sins? And if this is the case, why did God let my father die? Why didn't he intervene or send an angel? It doesn't make sense, and yet part of it does. It is this tangle—the shoulds and shouldn'ts, the rational and irrational—that seems to be the crux at the center of all the stories that the rabbi tells us. We live in a world where things make sense and don't make sense. Life is a puzzle. Years later, I come across these deceptively simple lines of a poem by the Israeli poet Yehuda Amichai. Its paradoxes fill me with curiosity and wonder. It reminds me of my wise rabbi whom I adored as a child, and who years later, officiated my wedding.

# MY CHILD BLOSSOMS SADLY

Yehuda Amichai (1924–2000)

Translated by Ruth Nevo

My child blossoms sadly.
He blossoms in spring without me,
he ripens in the sadness of my not being there.
I saw a cat playing with her kittens.
I shall not teach my son war,
I shall not teach him at all. I shall not be.
He puts sand in a small bucket.
He makes a sand cake.
I put sand in my body.
The cake crumbles. My body.

———

The Israeli poet Yehuda Amichai was born in Germany. He immigrated to Palestine with his Orthodox Jewish family in 1936 when he was twelve and Germany was under the control of Hitler. His poetry carries the anguished reverberations of history and politics. In an interview with *The Paris Review*, he reminds us that anti-Semitism predated Hitler in Germany. "We were called names. We had stones thrown at us. And, yes, this created real sorrow. We defended ourselves as well as we could. Funny thing, the common name we were called was Isaac—the way Muslims are called Ali or Mohammed. They'd call out, Isaac, go back to Palestine, leave our home, go to your place. They threw stones at us and shouted,

Go to Palestine." Growing up, Amichai went to synagogue once or sometimes twice a day. "I think religion is good for children, especially educated children, because it allows for imagination, a whole imaginative world apart from the practical world. The world of religion isn't a logical world; that's why children like it. It's a world of worked-out fantasies, very similar to children's stories or fairy tales." Amichai believed that poets must live in the experiential world and not close themselves off inside their studios.

This short, ten-line excerpt from a longer poem called "The Travels of the Last Benjamin of Tudela" is about the relationship between a father and a son. It could be Abraham and Isaac. It could be your father or your son. In the spaces between words we experience the passing of time and the legacy of generations and the paradox of instruction. Each passing day, a child grows older and his parents grow older. A father fears for his own demise and also his son's demise. On the surface the poem is about watching a child make cakes out of sand, but it also illustrates the threat of war and the potential destruction of a people. For me, it recalls days at the beach watching my own son build castles in the sand, or in the playground in the park, and how quickly our illusory sense of security faded the day the twin towers fell in New York City and the threat of war pressed closer to our shores. Amichai said in an interview: "I've often said that all poetry is political. This is because real poems deal with a human response to reality and politics is part of reality, history in the making. Even if a poet writes about sitting in a glass house drinking tea it reflects politics."

What does it mean to be Jewish? In graduate school, at the

University of Iowa's Writer's Workshop in Iowa City, I waitress weekends at a family-style barbecue place run by Midwestern farmers. One of the blond-haired, blue-eyed waitresses from Iowa City dressed in a red-and-white-checkered cowboy shirt with a bandana tied around her neck, tells me she'd never met a Jew before. Though she means no harm, I suddenly become aware of my dark hair and eyes, my eastern European blood, and its historical significance, and I feel a shudder of that recognition in my body. This poem reminds me of the meaning behind my inner tremble.

# PRAYER

## HAVE YOU PRAYED?
Li-Young Lee

I am young when my mother begins to date, and I worry about her. It seems as if every man who comes in sight of her wants her. And why shouldn't they? She's beautiful, with her long dark hair and curvy body. Even when we are at the grocery store, I see the way the men behind the meat counter stare at her, or the way the repairmen who come to fix our furnace or leaking pipes stay a little too long after they've finished to speak to her. What if something should happen to her and suddenly she was gone, like my father? I am plagued by the idea that I am doomed to become an orphan. I've come to think of it as an art, the way she carefully applies her makeup, pulls up her stockings that make her long legs look smooth and silky, puts her hair in big rollers so that once it's dry it falls in a luxurious flip against her shoulders. Once she leaves, her arm hooked in the arm of her date, I sit by my bedroom window and wait for her to get home. My heart leaps at any car that comes down our street and sinks when it passes by our house. As the minutes turn to hours, I become more anxious, convinced my mother has gotten into a car accident. Sometimes my imagination brings me to tears. It is no wonder that I identify with David Copperfield, Jane Eyre, Pippi Longstocking, and other orphaned children in literature. All children do. My favorite babysitter senses my unease. Before she tucks us into bed, she takes our hands and we all form a circle on the shag carpet of my bedroom floor. She teaches us the words to "Now I Lay Me Down to Sleep."

> Now I lay me down to sleep,
> I pray the Lord my soul to keep.
> If I should die before I wake
> I pray the Lord my soul to take.

At the end of the prayer we say aloud the names of everyone we know and care about—our mother, our father in heaven, our aunts, uncles, and cousins—and every time we think we have exhausted the list, one of us suddenly blurts out a name we have forgotten, and slowly, aware I am not alone, my fear subsides.

In bed, after our babysitter closes the door and sister number three has fallen asleep in the bed across from mine, I silently continue to recite the prayer whose origins come directly from the Bible. Before I understand what is real, what is not real, and what I only wish for, I believe that the soul of my own father is with the Lord watching over my family, and I can feel the essence of my father in the musty air of our small bedroom. I pray he will look after my mother and return her safely home.

# HAVE YOU PRAYED?

Li-Young Lee (1957–)

When the wind
turns and asks, in my father's voice,
*Have you prayed?*

I know three things. One:
I'm never finished answering to the dead.

Two: A man is four winds and three fires.
And the four winds are his father's voice,
his mother's voice . . .

Or maybe he's seven winds and ten fires.
And the fires are seeing, hearing, touching,
dreaming, thinking . . .
Or is he the breath of God?

When the wind turns traveler
and asks, in my father's voice, *Have you prayed?*
I remember three things.
One: A father's love

is milk and sugar,
two-thirds worry, two-thirds grief, and what's left over

is trimmed and leavened to make the bread
the dead and the living share.

And patience? That's to endure
the terrible leavening and kneading.

And wisdom? That's my father's face in sleep.

When the wind
asks, *Have you prayed?*
I know it's only me

reminding myself
a flower is one station between
earth's wish and earth's rapture, and blood

was fire, salt, and breath long before
it quickened any wand or branch, any limb
that woke speaking. It's just me

in the gowns of the wind,
or my father through me, asking,
*Have you found your refuge yet?*
asking, *Are you happy?*

Strange. A troubled father. A happy son.
The wind with a voice. And me talking to no one.

———

Li-Young Lee was born in Indonesia to Chinese exiles. In
reading his call-to-prayer-like poem, I remember the nights
I lay in bed reciting "Now I Lay Me Down to Sleep," a clas-

sic children's bedtime prayer from the eighteenth century. Prayer offers a door to a place where we surrender our literal and rational minds and embrace faith. In "Have You Prayed?" Li-Young Lee equates prayer and the spiritual world with his father and his ancestors before him. Though written across cultures and time, both prayer-poems invite us to abandon ourselves to the unknown and the dead.

In reading "Have You Prayed?" I don't attempt to parse it literally. Instead I allow its seductive voice to take me to the enchantments of the unknown world where father, legacy, and prayer are all intertwined. Surely this is one of the reasons poetry enriches us. A poem links us to a universe at once intimate and communal. Poets and artists work in solitude and by intuition. They have the same mission: to capture and fathom the reality beyond appearances, the world invisible to the eye.

# IMAGINATION

## THE SNOW MAN
### Wallace Stevens

In Cleveland, Ohio, the winters are snow-filled and cold. Sometimes there is so much ice on the windows we can barely see out, and the snow is more than a foot deep. And what else is there to do on those snowy days when school is canceled except go outside and build a snowman? While my mother is still in bed, my sisters and I come downstairs and stare out our frosty windows at all the snow covering our lawn, tree branches, and bushes in a white shroud. We put on our snow jackets and leggings, hats and boots and mittens, and run outside, where the snow has not yet been tainted. We roll a small mound of packed snow across our front lawn until it grows in circumference and girth, first one ball and then the other, to form the snowman's body and head. There is something eerie and subversive in the act: how we ransack the once untouched snow-covered lawn and leave it trodden and raw, exposing patches of grass and mud, to make the body of the snowman. Then we go back inside, trudging snow onto the carpet, cheeks burning from the cold, our mother still asleep in bed upstairs, and gather charcoal for eyes, a carrot for a nose, and a box of the Sunkist raisins our mother fills our pockets with before we go to school, to create a row of raisins in the shape of a smile. What is this need in us to transform snow into our own likeness? Is it that same impulse and urgency an artist encounters when she creates a work of art? Sometimes, after we finish building our snowman I stop for a moment. The wind burns my cheeks and I listen to its sound, which is almost like a voice, and it fills me with the mystery of the universe, that mystical sensation that makes me wonder: Why am I here? Who are we? How did we come to being? It's still early in the morning and the snow hasn't stopped. It's so white and bright, I can barely see. It is no wonder that I am enchanted and puzzled by Wallace Stevens's poem "The Snow Man" the first time I read it.

## THE SNOW MAN
### Wallace Stevens (1879–1955)

One must have a mind of winter
To regard the frost and the boughs
Of the pine-trees crusted with snow;

And have been cold a long time
To behold the junipers shagged with ice,
The spruces rough in the distant glitter

Of the January sun; and not to think
Of any misery in the sound of the wind,
In the sound of a few leaves,

Which is the sound of the land
Full of the same wind
That is blowing in the same bare place

For the listener, who listens in the snow,
And, nothing himself, beholds
Nothing that is not there and the nothing that is.

———

In his essay "The Necessary Angel," the American modernist poet Wallace Stevens wrote, "unreal things have a reality of their own, in poetry as elsewhere. We do not hesitate, in poetry, to yield ourselves to the unreal, when it is possible to yield ourselves." This quote is a perfect introduction to understanding his poetics.

"The Snow Man," a beautiful elegy to childhood, perhaps draws on the iconic association of building a snowman as a child. Our reading of a poem reflects our own personal identification with the images and narrative the poem evokes within us. The snowman of the poem personifies the child in existential thought, seeing the world released from his parents' reflection, aware suddenly both of his own insignificance and importance. Like layers of snow mounting in a field, "The Snow Man," embracing abstraction, inhabits several realms of reality: the reality of what is seen, and what is not seen in our imagination. Who isn't enchanted by a ghostly snowman on a lawn in winter?

Of this poem Wallace Stevens said in a letter: "I shall explain 'The Snow Man' as an example of the necessity of identifying oneself with reality in order to understand it and enjoy it."

Years later, when my son is small and he and I build his first snowman together, I think of all those snow-filled winters with my sisters, when we stayed outside for hours, licking the rusty taste of snow from our mittens, and of course, of this poem. The poem unites us. We are all essentially alone, and yet also part of a larger humanity. An idea no better stated then in those last paradoxical and haunting lines:

> For the listener, who listens in the snow,
> And, nothing himself, beholds
> Nothing that that is not there and the nothing that is.

# DEATH

## STOPPING BY WOODS ON
## A SNOWY EVENING
### Robert Frost

As a young child I fail to make the connection that individuals composed nursery rhymes, songs, poems, and stories, some of which I knew by heart. In my own fantasy, I imagine that poems, songs, and stories came out of the mouth of God. When I discover that an actual person took pen to paper, and through invention and imagination created a work of art, I wonder: Could I do that too? In sixth grade, writing in those blue books our teachers give us to take our written exams, I attempt my first novel, a story about a girl running away from home. It is here I learn a lesson of a lifetime. Stories are born from desires we are too afraid to act out in real life.

In my fourth grade classroom, along with memorizing "The Road Not Taken," we study other poems by Robert Frost: "Stopping by Woods on a Snowy Evening," "Birches," and "After Apple Picking." Through Frost's poetry, I am privy to the tough pulse of another being's consciousness. I enjoy how each poem tells a micro-story. In "Stopping by Woods on a Snowy Evening," I relate to the eerie quiet of a winter night as the narrator stops his sleigh to watch the snow falling in the woods. In "Birches," my spirit rises to the tops of those trees. I am at one with the splendor of the boy "whose only play was what he found himself," bending the birch's limbs.

I'm enchanted by trees and their humanlike qualities and am seduced by the meditative mood of the poem and its plaintive storytelling. Miss Hudson tells us about Robert Frost's life and that he had read a poem for President John F. Kennedy's inauguration in 1961. I love listening to his impassioned speeches on our black-and-white television set with its rabbit-ear antenna. After Kennedy was shot and killed, I, a girl of six, sat in our den with my mother and sisters, watching his funeral procession, my mother in tears. It was the first time I witnessed a funeral procession and I forever associated it with my own father's early death. Throughout the day, the pierce of our private and communal loss resided in the dark and drafty den of our house. Robert Frost was one of Kennedy's favorite poets, and at the president's funeral, Sid Davis of Westinghouse Broadcasting ended his report with a fitting passage from "Stopping by Woods on a Snowy Evening," as the poem suggests the tragic premature end to a great man who certainly had "miles to go" before the eternal sleep of death.

## STOPPING BY WOODS ON A SNOWY EVENING
### Robert Frost

Whose woods these are I think I know.
His house is in the village though;
He will not see me stopping here
To watch his woods fill up with snow.

My little horse must think it queer
To stop without a farmhouse near
Between the woods and frozen lake
The darkest evening of the year.

He gives his harness bells a shake
To ask if there is some mistake.
The only other sound's the sweep
Of easy wind and downy flake.

The woods are lovely, dark and deep,
But I have promises to keep,
And miles to go before I sleep,
And miles to go before I sleep.

———

"Stopping by Woods on a Snowy Evening" was the first poem my son memorized when he was a young boy. We read it together before bedtime from a beautifully illustrated children's book. He wrote a poem of his own mimicking its rhythms he called "The Children of Riverside." Frost believed a poet didn't have to suffer while writing a poem. He enjoyed its theatrical nature. "So many talk, I wonder how falsely, about what it costs them, what agony it is to write. I've often been quoted: 'No tears in the writer, no tears in the reader. No surprise for the writer, no surprise for the reader.' But another distinction I made is: however sad, no grievance, grief without grievance. How could I, how could anyone have a good time with what cost me too much agony, how could they? What do I want to communicate but what a *hell* of a good time I had writing it? The whole thing is performance and prowess and feats of association."

The easy cadences in the poem are reminiscent of nursery rhymes, and its end rhymes give the poem its musical quality. Each stanza is made up of four lines, each line iambic (a poetic term that describes the particular rhythm that the words establish in that line), with four stressed syllables. Within each stanza, the first, second, and fourth lines rhyme. The third line does not rhyme, but the end word sets up the rhyme for the following stanza. The rhymes make the poem easy to memorize. On the surface, the poem is seductively simple. The speaker stops by the woods on a snowy evening. He is taken in by the scenery, wants to stay, but other obligations force him to move on as he also becomes aware of how many more miles he must travel before reaching his destination. "The woods are lovely, dark, and deep," tells us that there is more going on in the poem than a man traveling from one destination to another. The poem invites us to ponder death and to think of how much time we have left and how we might experience that time. We can experience the poem on its surface, charms alone, or travel deeper as if through layers of snow, and find other meanings in it, including some uniquely our own. Robert Frost wrote, "Poetry is a way of taking life by the throat."

# POETRY

## ARS POETICA?
Czesław Miłosz

I try to be a good child. I do my homework. I struggle not to fight with my sisters. I help my mother. On her birthday, I enlist my sisters' assistance and together we take out the mop and vacuum cleaner, scrub the kitchen counters, fluff the pillows on the sofa, and clean the entire house until the floors and countertops sparkle. And when my mother comes down the stairs, Queen of the Night, she gasps in delight and surprise. When I am fourteen, I babysit for pocket money. I babysit for the little deaf girl who lives down our block, for the twin boys two blocks over, for the baby next door. After I read my charges their stories, give them their cookies and milk, and tuck them into bed, I turn on the TV or talk to one of my girlfriends on the phone. Sometimes the night seems to go on forever. Restless, I raid the fridge and roam the house. I run my fingers along spines of books on the shelves in the library. Flip through magazines. Open closets just to peek, wander into master bedrooms. One night I find myself in the en suite bathroom—the size of my bedroom at home—belonging to one of the more glamorous mothers in the neighborhood. On top of the vanity sits a tray filled with her powders, lotions, lipstick tubes, and perfumes. I look at my unpleasant face in the mirror, and on a lark, try on a pink lipstick. I hear the car pull up the driveway and quickly slip the tube into my jean's pocket, wipe my lips with a Kleenex, and fly down the stairs before the front-door lock turns. After I am paid and sent on my way, I feel the stolen lipstick tube practically burning a hole in my jeans' pocket. For nights I stay up, unable to sleep. Who am I? I feel so ashamed. It's as if I am two people, and more than I know of myself. When I am called back to babysit the following Saturday—my heart beating—I bring the lipstick with me and return it to the tray on the vanity where I found it, but still I am haunted by the way in which my desires fly out without my will to control them. This poem, about the nature of poetry and more, recalls that time, and that contract I broke with myself that filled me with shame.

## ARS POETICA?
Czesław Miłosz (1911–2004)
Translated by Czesław Miłosz and Lillian Vallee

I have always aspired to a more spacious form
that would be free from the claims of poetry or prose
and would let us understand each other without exposing
the author or reader to sublime agonies.

In the very essence of poetry there is something indecent:
a thing is brought forth which we didn't know we had in us,

so we blink our eyes, as if a tiger had sprung out
and stood in the light, lashing his tail.

That's why poetry is rightly said to be dictated by a daimonion,
though it's an exaggeration to maintain that he must be an
     angel.
It's hard to guess where that pride of poets comes from,
when so often they're put to shame by the disclosure of
     their frailty.

What reasonable man would like to be a city of demons,
who behave as if they were at home, speak in many tongues,
and who, not satisfied with stealing his lips or hand,
work at changing his destiny for their convenience?

It's true that what is morbid is highly valued today,
and so you may think that I am only joking
or that I've devised just one more means
of praising Art with the help of irony.

There was a time when only wise books were read,
helping us to bear our pain and misery.
This, after all, is not quite the same
as leafing through a thousand works fresh from psychiatric
     clinics.

And yet the world is different from what it seems to be
and we are other than how we see ourselves in our ravings.
People therefore preserve silent integrity,
thus earning the respect of their relatives and neighbors.

The purpose of poetry is to remind us
how difficult it is to remain just one person,
for our house is open, there are no keys in the doors,
and invisible guests come in and out at will.

What I'm saying here is not, I agree, poetry,
as poems should be written rarely and reluctantly,
under unbearable duress and only with the hope
that good spirits, not evil ones, choose us for their
    instrument.

———

"Ars Poetica," a term that means *the art of poetry* or *on the art of poetry*, is derived from Horace's "Ars Poetica," one of the first known treatises on poetry, written between 20 and 13 B.C.E. Horace's poem sketches what he understood as the principles of poetry, which include art, decorum, sincerity, and purpose. In Miłosz's "Ars Poetica?"—a title ending with a question mark—he calls into question the original principles of an "Ars Poetica" by establishing that it should push past the boundaries between prose and poetry. He advocates for a poetry that sets out to discover what is indecent in us. Through exposing indecency—the unsayable—a transaction is offered to the reader. We only know it when, like "a tiger sprung out," it lashes its tail and frightens us to attention. The first time I read "Ars Poetica?" I am reminded of the shameful incident in which my own sense of morality was tested. Essential poems expose what we are afraid of most, even what we find indecent in ourselves.

And when we read such a poem, we are reminded of our own indecency.

When Czesław Miłosz was asked what kind of philosophy he finds appropriate for his poetry, he replied: "There are some kinds of philosophy that remind me of the circumstance of driving at night and having a hare jump in front of the lights. The hare doesn't know how to get out of the beam of light, he runs straight ahead. I am interested in the kind of philosophy that would be useful to the hare in that instance." In other words, he strove philosophically to write poems immediate and potent enough to save the hare.

Emily Dickinson famously said in regard to her own definition of poetry: "If I read a book and it makes my whole body so cold no fire can warm me I know *that* is poetry. If I feel physically as if the top of my head were taken off, I know *that* is poetry. These are the only ways I know it. Is there any other way?"

# FAMILY

JANUARY 1, 1965
Joseph Brodsky
CHILDHOOD
Rainer Maria Rilke

Old-world traits such as modesty, fear of standing out, insecurity, and distrust are part of my inheritance from my mother's ancestors, who grew up in Eastern Europe and immigrated to America. After World War I and the mass exodus of emigration, the children of immigrants in Cleveland, like in other cities in America, eventually moved up into the middle class, creating new institutions—synagogue centers, progressive Hebrew schools, Jewish community centers—attempting to assimilate and Americanize while at home there still lingered a feeling of difference. My great aunts and grandparents referred to anyone who wasn't Jewish as a Gentile. You were one or the other. There was a hierarchy among Jewish immigrant families. Men worked in the garment districts, or as tailors or peddlers; my paternal grandfather opened a pawn shop, my mother's father worked as a bank teller; women prepared the meals and took care of the children; and children were coddled. Fear lurked over our shoulders. Fear that history would repeat itself and all our ancestors had built, if they were not cautious, would be taken away.

I too am raised in this atmosphere of stuffy seclusion and distrust. All the rooms in my grandfather's house, where we go every Friday night for Shabbat, seem too small. There are doilies on the cherry wood tables that slip off if I lean on them. Prayer books, antique clocks, and tchotchkes from the old country don the shelves, mantles, and walls. I'm afraid I'll break something if I'm not careful. Sometimes around my relatives I can't breathe. My maternal great aunts are protective of us. They worry in the winter when we come to see them that we are not dressed warmly enough. They worry about the crosswalk across the street from our school and whether we'll get run down if we don't carefully look both ways. They think we are too thin or too plump. Protectiveness breeds fear and distrust. Being raised without a father perpetuates this fear. There is always the sense that instability and ruin are right around the corner. I am aware that being Jewish makes me different and am grateful that my face is not marked by typical Jewish features: big nose and kinky hair.

Once on Passover, I notice an extra place set at the table and a goblet of wine later poured, though no one drank it. At first I think that it is for a guest who has not arrived and then I think to myself maybe my father hasn't died at all, maybe it has all been a terrible lie or a trick and this cup of wine is for him and soon he will be home. My imagination runs wild. Later, in Hebrew school, I learn that the common tradition at a Seder is to have an empty cup for the prophet Elijah, which, at the end of the Seder, is filled with wine. During the Pass-over Seder we recount in the Haggadah the redemption of the Jews from Egypt and also express our hope for future re-demption with the coming of the Messiah. The tradition is that Elijah the prophet, in his eventual coming, will be the one to announce the coming of the Messiah. No matter. In my mind, my father has become my own Jewish prophet. One day he will come. I am sure of it.

At the table we listen to the grown-ups talk while feeling squirrely in our creaky, wooden fold-up chairs, overheated from the cooking of brisket and potatoes that hangs heavy in the air. One uncle talks about a friend who was overlooked for a promotion because he was Jewish. My aunt won't serve the challah because my grandfather bought it at the grocery store instead of the Jewish bakery. "Is he Jewish?" another aunt prods my mother when she speaks about someone new she is dating. For my thirteenth birthday, I am given a gold Jewish star necklace as a present but I'm afraid to wear it out-side my shirt. I don't quite understand the obsession with being Jewish. It seems to be a blessing and a curse.

At school, I don't like being the object of other people's attention. I don't know how to talk to adults. I bury my head in my books and rarely raise my hand or speak unless I am called on. In this way, I learn how easy and more comfortable it is to slip below the radar of authority. I don't trust teachers or adults in general. If a teacher speaks to me or gives me at-tention, no matter how kind, I read pity in her eyes. Pity to have lost a father, pity to have to write a card to her grandfa-ther instead of her father for Father's Day. Pity morphs into a lack of trust. If a teacher praises an essay or paper I write, I can't take in the praise, and instead tell myself he or she just feels sorry for me. It's not a great way of being, but I don't know how to be anyone else. Why am I this way? Why this fear of stepping out? Of being known? This fear of happiness? Like many girls my age, I eventually read *The Diary of Anne Frank* and her story makes my blood run cold. I think how lucky she is to have been in seclusion, not just with her family but with Peter's family, and I am eager to skip to the parts in the diary where I anticipate Anne and Peter will have their first kiss. But, mostly, each page I turn leaves me with a pit in my stomach. Will this legacy of fear and hiding repeat itself?

## JANUARY 1, 1965

### Joseph Brodsky (1940–1996)

The kings will lose your old address.
No star will flare up to impress.
The ear may yield, under duress,
to blizzards' nagging roar.
The shadows falling off your back,
you'd snuff the candle, hit the sack,
for calendars more nights can pack
than there are candles for.

What is this? Sadness? Yes, perhaps.
A little tune that never stops.
One knows by heart its downs and ups.
May it be played on par

with things to come, with one's eclipse,
as gratefulness of eyes and lips
for what occasionally keeps
them trained on something far.

And staring up where no cloud drifts
because your sock's devoid of gifts
you'll understand this thrift: it fits
your age; it's not a slight.
It is too late for some breakthrough,
for miracles, for Santa's crew.
And suddenly you'll realize that you
yourself are a gift outright.

———

The more I read the poem, the further I read into it my own inheritance. "What is this? Sadness?" this poem asks. It is a poem of exile, opening with images of the Wise Men, the Kings who have forgotten one's address and a star, perhaps the Jewish Star of David or Shield of David, with its hexagram shape that dates to the seventeenth century, "that will not flare up to impress." Joseph Brodsky, born a Russian Jew and once a lauded poet in his homeland, was eventually persecuted for his fiery and individualistic poetry that challenged Soviet ideals. After standing trial for "parasitism" he was forced to live in a hard labor camp and then a mental institution until American intellectuals helped get him released. He came to America in 1972 with the help of the poet W. H. Auden to teach at the University of Michigan.

"January 1, 1965" was written while Brodsky was in internal exile enduring hard labor in Norenskaia, in the Arkhangelsk region of northern Russia. In the Soviet Union, New Year's celebrations came to be seen as a substitute for Christmas. Every year, Brodsky wrote a new year's poem. "January 1, 1965" acknowledges the passing of time as represented in the opening stanza by the image of candles, the calendar, and the lurking fear of death. It contains allusions of oppression and persecution. Tones of resignation reverberate; the poet is too old to celebrate "Santa" and believe in miracles. His stockings are empty. "Devoid of gifts." Ironically, Brodsky was only twenty-four when he wrote the poem. Even with its defiant note in the last line, "you realize you yourself are a gift outright," the futility of escaping history is omnipresent. Though my ancestors were not exiled in this way, the aftershocks of being born a Jew and the legacy of oppression were part of my historical inheritance.

We rarely know how or why certain events and experiences shape us in childhood or the way in which we absorb the atmosphere in ways that linger.

## CHILDHOOD
### Rainer Maria Rilke (1874–1926)
### Translated by Joseph Cadora

Best to often recall—before we try
to search among such abandoned ruins—
those lingering childhood afternoons
that will never return, and then to ask why.

Still they call out to us, perhaps in the rain,
but what this might mean we no longer know;
meetings, comings and goings—never again
with these things did life seem to overflow,

since nothing ever happened to us then,
except what happens to animals or things,
and we felt then as something quite human,
what was theirs—filled to the brim with imaginings.

And we were prone to a shepherd's loneliness,
and so filled with great distances then,
summoned from afar and rapturous
while, slowly as a growing thread of yarn,
into that picture sequence we were drawn—
which, when we dwell on it now, baffles us.

———

Rilke was fascinated with exploring childhood: its loneliness, the sense of time passing, and its mysterious effect on character in his poetry. Like it was for many of us, childhood was a difficult time for Rilke. He was fragile and effeminate; his mother had wanted a girl and dressed him as one. His father was a civil servant, and his parents enrolled him in military school hoping he would become an officer—a highly unlikely profession for such a sensitive young man. It wasn't until many years later, with the help of an uncle, that he left the military academy and pursued an education that would enable him to prepare for university and a literary career.

Many of the images of childhood in his poems are inspired by his own memories. In the poem "Childhood," Rilke describes how nothing really happens to us in childhood ("except what happens to animals and things"), with its implication that as children we are subjected to the whims and decisions of our parents or guardians. Of course this is meant ironically because these *things* have a profound impact on us, even though as children we don't yet know it. In Letter 6 in his prose work, *Letters to a Young Poet*, an essential companion for any aspiring artist, Rilke writes of the loneliness, confusion, and solitude of childhood, and solitude's necessity in forming an internal and creative life. It is that potent combination from which our consciousness evolves.

Rome
December 23, 1903

My dear Mr. Kappus,

You shall not be without a greeting from me when Christmas comes and when you, in the midst of the holiday, are bearing your solitude more heavily than usual. But if then you notice that it is great, rejoice because of this: for what task (ask yourself) would solitude be that had no greatness; there is but *one* solitude, and that is great, and not easy to bear, and to almost everybody come hours when they would gladly exchange it for any sort of intercourse, however banal and cheap, for the semblance of some slight accord with the first comer, with the unworthiest. . . . But perhaps those are the very hours when solitude grows, for its growing is painful as the growing of boys and sad as the beginning of springtimes. But that must not mislead you. The necessary thing is after all but this: solitude, great, inner solitude. Going-into-oneself and for hours meeting no one—this one must be able to attain. To be solitary, the way one was solitary as a child, when the grownups went around involved with things that seemed important and big because they themselves looked so busy and because one comprehended nothing of their doings.

# FATHERS

## THOSE WINTER SUNDAYS
Robert Hayden

When I am in the fifth grade, my mother greets us when we come home from school, and before we can put down our books and rush into the kitchen for a snack, she ushers us upstairs to her bedroom and announces that she is married. She holds out her hand and shows us an opal-and-gold ring and gives each of us a hug. Where was the wedding? I wonder. Why were we not invited? She tells us they went to the courthouse and the justice of the peace performed the ceremony. That phrase stays in my memory. Who is this justice? And what does it mean? And who is this man who is now her husband? This moment marks a turning point in my life. Now there is a man downstairs who plans to move into our house, inhabited only by young girls and a woman. With our brushes, combs, hair clips, and crèmes in the bathrooms, my mother's closets in the master bedroom filled to bursting with her dresses and shoes, her bedroom smelling like Chanel No. 5 and hairspray. I don't know how he'll fit in. Even the ceilings and alcoves seem too low for what we will soon discover is his over six-foot-tall frame. In a matter of hours everything changes. No more slumber parties stretched out on our mother's king-size bed in flannel nightgowns watching *Father Knows Best* or *Dick Van Dyke* and eating bowls of Jiffy Pop while our mother gets ready for her date. There is a handsome man downstairs with two suitcases, we are told, who is waiting to welcome us as our new dad. Why didn't we get to choose, I wonder? We soon learn that he's Irish Catholic. I consider if my relatives will approve and if that is why my mother eloped, but this is not something ever spoken of.

During the first few months of the new arrangement, it seems as if we are rehearsing for this new role of family. It is important to be on good behavior. Gone are the simple dinners of peanut butter and jelly sandwiches and heated SpaghettiOs from a can, Sloppy Joes, grilled cheese sandwiches, tuna noodle casserole, and wiener goulash. Gone are the TV dinners my mother popped in the oven when she was readying for a date. I like Salisbury steak, with its little tin of mashed potatoes and peas. Sister number three prefers the fried chicken, and sister number one likes turkey and gravy with its cavity of cranberry sauce. Now the refrigerator is filled with expensive meats and cheeses, and my mother's new bible is Julia Child's *Mastering the Art of French Cooking*.

I like this new version of my mother, but there's a slight desperation in her need to please. Instead of TV dinners and heated cans, my mother makes thick steaks and too-rare roast beef for dinner and slaves for hours to bake fresh almond cakes. On Sundays, I go to the bakery with my stepfather and together we pick out a box of jelly, chocolate, and glazed donuts so buttery they melt in our mouth. This new father likes his girls to dress alike when he takes us out to dinner. One day he takes us to Saks Fifth Avenue and buys us three of the same red-and-black checkered dresses. Not only are there new meals on the table but my mother comes to life in a different way. Every Saturday she goes to the beauty parlor to get her hair and nails done, and they go out. Sundays she cooks all day. Sometimes I watch my stepfather creep into the kitchen and kiss my mother's neck when she's huddled over the stove.

The honeymoon period lasts a year or so before their spontaneous decision to marry begins to show its seams. My stepfather travels during the week, and when he comes home, he prepares himself a scotch on the rocks and sits in the new black leather Eames chair he had delivered when he moved in to watch the game or read the paper. He looks tired. God knows what he does when he's away from us. God knows if he had any idea how deep the footprints were he would be required to fill, that of a husband and father to a household long in want and need.

The strange world of husbands and wives is confusing. Sometimes he doesn't come home from work till almost dawn and I hear my mother crying in her bed. The next morning they fight all day. My sisters and I seclude ourselves in the basement playing Candyland or Monopoly where all you have to do is roll the dice or twirl the spinner to determine your fate. It seems so simple, but it's not. Through the floorboards that vibrate underneath his heavy walk, I feel my stepfather's terrible power over my mother and hence over all of us. All I want is for them to stop fighting. Sometimes I even blame my mother. The next morning I slowly creep down the stairs. My mother is still sleeping. My stepfather is awake. I hear him in the cold kitchen and slowly my breathing returns to normal. I am certain that our well-being depends on his being there.

## THOSE WINTER SUNDAYS
### Robert Hayden (1913–1980)

Sundays too my father got up early
and put his clothes on in the blueblack cold,
then with cracked hands that ached
from labor in the weekday weather made
banked fires blaze. No one ever thanked him.

I'd wake and hear the cold splintering, breaking.
When the rooms were warm, he'd call,
and slowly I would rise and dress,
fearing the chronic angers of that house,

Speaking indifferently to him,
who had driven out the cold
and polished my good shoes as well.
What did I know, what did I know
of love's austere and lonely offices?

———

The landscape rendered in a poem through its specific narrative—a memory of a boy getting up on a Sunday to the crackling of a fire roaring in the fireplace made by his father to keep his family warm—has the ability to be universal and cut across cultures, religions, and economic backgrounds. Robert Hayden grew up in a Detroit working-class neighborhood whose specifics—"cracked hands that ached from labor"—inform "Those Winter Sundays." His parents separated before he was born and he was raised by foster parents in a turbulent home marked by verbal and physical abuse. Shades of the trauma he sustained as a child resonate throughout his poetic oeuvre. Be that as it may, "Those Winter Sundays," evokes memories and reverberations of the complicated "austere and lonely offices" of a collective childhood, whether rich or poor, where a father wields his tender and cruel power.

# FAITH

AFTER GREAT PAIN A
FORMAL FEELING COMES,
I'M NOBODY WHO ARE YOU,
and "HOPE" IS A THING WITH FEATHERS
Emily Dickinson

As a private and bookish adolescent, I retreat inside Louisa May Alcott's *Little Women* seeking refuge in another time and place. The novel follows the lives of four sisters—Meg, Jo, Beth, and Amy March—narrating their passage from childhood to womanhood. Their father is away from home fighting in the Civil War. The novel depicts what it is like to grow up in a household of women. For obvious reasons, this book speaks to me. I read it after school, I read it in the morning. I read it late into the night when the moon presses its light against the pane of my window. I read it in the library at school until the dog-eared pages hold my finger marks, jottings in the margins, and my spills of tea. Why do I love it so? It makes me believe that maybe one day I might be like Jo, my favorite character in the novel who wants to become a writer. I dream and fantasize that one day soon this might happen to me, and with my books I might be able to support my mother and sisters. That book held power in its pages. Later I discover Laura Ingalls Wilder and her adventurous stories of settling on the wild prairie, Jane Austen's *Pride and Prejudice* about a mother and her many daughters, and Emily Brontë's *Wuthering Heights* and its dark reverberations of eternal love. Edith Wharton's *Ethan Frome,* a love story about a terrible accident, keeps me up for nights. For a week I am inseparable from my copy of *The Red Pony.* I ingest novels and stories by Dickens and Tolstoy and later Dostoevsky and Chekhov, and the characters in these different worlds inform my envy, my empathy, my courage, my consciousness.

One day in our school library, I roam the poetry shelf and discover a large volume of poetry filled with untitled poems identified by first lines and Roman numbers. The poems belong to the American poet Emily Dickinson and I identify with them immediately. It is as if I opened a box that held my private secrets and desires. I love the playful, spirited surfaces of the poems similar to the verse of Robert Louis Stevenson. But they resonate with deep undertones about abstract concepts like love, hope, faith, and death. It makes me feel smart to think I understand them. Once I learn more of Emily Dickinson's biography and her reclusive lifestyle, I am more enchanted. How is it possible that this poet, who had expected to become "the belle of Amherst when I reach my seventeenth year," ended up a reclusive poet who had "not been outside her house in fifteen years." It amazes me that a person who lived in seclusion could know so much about human nature. Since I was only two years old when my father died, I had always associated his loss through the world of my mother—it was her grief, not mine. Losing him meant my life was different. But reading Dickinson's poetry in a little cubbyhole in the library of my school I let the dark undercurrent of loss pulsate in my own life and unleash a well of sorrow. It was as if I too were frozen, my heart stiff, ceremonious, living a mechanical existence. Suddenly a formal feeling pervades my being.

## AFTER GREAT PAIN, A FORMAL FEELING COMES (341)
### Emily Dickinson (1830–1886)

After great pain, a formal feeling comes —
The Nerves sit ceremonious, like Tombs —
The stiff Heart questions was it He, that bore
And Yesterday, or Centuries before?

The Feet, mechanical, go round —
Of Ground, or Air, or Ought —
A Wooden way
Regardless grown,
A Quartz contentment, like a stone —

This is the Hour of Lead —
Remembered, if outlived,
As Freezing persons, recollect the Snow —
First—Chill—then Stupor—then the letting go —

———

Many years later when I am in my twenties I come across a book called *On Death and Dying* by the Swiss psychologist Elisabeth Kübler-Ross. In the pages she posits a model of grief that consists of five stages: denial, anger, bargaining, depression, and acceptance. I am reminded of Emily Dickinson's poem "After great pain, a formal feeling comes" and recall the simplicity of its portrayal of grief through the use of four words: "chill," "stupor," "letting go." "A formal feeling" depicts that changed state obtained after having survived the death of an intimate. Now whenever I think of grief or suffering after a terrible event, I think of it as "the Hour of Lead."

Emily Dickinson never knew literary success in her lifetime, publishing only twelve of nearly 1,800 poems. Her close family and few friends and acquaintances "had an enormous impact on her verse." She wrote to Reverend Charles Wadsworth after reading a piece he wrote in *The Atlantic Monthly* and they began more than a decade of correspondence. Wadsworth visited her home in 1860, and again just one other time, and many critics believe that the tone of wistfulness and longing in her verse was generated by his absence. From that time, Dickinson lived in almost total isolation from the outside world, speaking to acquaintances sometimes from behind a closed door. And yet behind that closed door was a desk, shelves of books, an ink pen, and paper. Poetry gave her solitary life purpose and meaning. In her sharp, clever, eccentric poems we discover a voice that embraced difficult and complicated circumstances. But her verse—whimsical, artfully composed—is also infused with optimism and faith. Her lines are clear and concise, distinguished by rhyme, sound, punctuated with her signature dash and exclamation marks, half-rhymes and surprising line breaks. Life, time, nature, grief, eternity are her themes. She accepted her private isolation and agoraphobia and chose to commune with humanity through her poems.

## I'M NOBODY! WHO ARE YOU? (288)
### Emily Dickinson

I'm Nobody! Who are you?
Are you—Nobody—Too?
Then there's a pair of us!
Don't tell! they'd advertise—you know!

How dreary—to be—Somebody!
How public—like a Frog —
To tell one's name—the Livelong June —
To an admiring Bog!

Brenda Wineapple, in her prize-winning work of nonfiction, *White Heat: The Friendship of Emily Dickinson and Thomas Wentworth Higginson*, writes of Dickinson's verse: "And when we turn to her poems, we find that they too, like her life, stop the narrative. Lyric outbursts, they tell no tales about who did what to whom in the habitable world. Rather, they whisper their wisdom from deep, very deep, within ourselves. And perhaps these poems plunge down so far—perhaps they unsettle us so—because Dickinson writes of experiences that we, who live in time, can hardly name."

Dickinson said in a letter to her friends Elizabeth and Josiah Holland: "Perhaps you laugh at me! Perhaps the whole United States are laughing at me too! . . . I can't stop for that! My business is to love. I found a bird this morning down—down on a little bush at the foot of the garden and wherefore sing, I said, since nobody hears? One sob in the throat, one flutter of bosom—'My business is to sing—and away she rose!' "

## "HOPE" IS THE THING WITH FEATHERS (254)
### Emily Dickinson

"Hope" is the thing with feathers —
That perches in the soul —
And sings the tune without the words —
And never stops—at all —

And sweetest—in the Gale—is heard —
And sore must be the storm —
That could abash the little Bird
That kept so many warm —

I've heard it in the chillest land —
And on the strangest Sea —
Yet,—never,—in Extremity,
It asked a crumb—of Me.

Hope is like a bird that perches inside us. It keeps us warm. It never asks anything of us. No one can fully destroy it. It sings a tune without words. In Dickinson's eccentric hands, it becomes ordinary, intimate, familiar as a crumb from a slice of bread. Perhaps that is why Dickinson's poems are relatable. They express sentiments of inadequacy, loss, feelings of despair. Even though Dickinson lived much of her life in seclusion, at her very heart she was a dreamer and many of her poems echo promise and possibility. "'Hope' is the thing with feathers" acknowledges the enduring human capability for hope. And hope she did that her verse would meet the approval of Mr. Thomas Wentworth Higginson.

MR. HIGGINSON,
—Are you too deeply occupied to say if my verse is alive?
The mind is so near itself it cannot see distinctly— and I have none to ask.
Should you think it breathed, and had you the leisure to tell me, I should feel quick gratitude.
If I make the mistake, that you dared to tell me would give me sincerer honor toward you.
I inclose my name, asking you, if you please, sir, to tell me what is true?
That you will not betray me it is needless to ask, since honor is its own pawn.

# FOREBODING

## MY PAPA'S WALTZ
### Theodore Roethke

Hope arrives with my mother's pregnancy, her fourth, and the arrival of our new baby sister. Hope not only for my parents' marriage but also for a new future for all of us, and in my baby sister's early infancy, our house comes to life again. Our new baby is like Dickinson's little bird, "sweetest—in the Gale," offering a new chance at happiness. We fight over who gets to feed her a bottle or change her diaper. She has my stepfather's blond hair, blue eyes, fair complexion, and warm and cheery disposition. But nevertheless, everything is topsy-turvy. For one, our house with three bedrooms upstairs is suddenly too small. We turn the downstairs den into a bedroom so that the baby has her own nursery upstairs. My mother buys her a wooden cradle from an antique shop because she reads that babies need a closed space to mimic the womb. She buys an antique rocking chair, and at night when we rock the baby to sleep and feed her a bottle she puts a record of lullabies on the turntable.

"Bye, bye baby bunting, daddies gone a hunting," resonates throughout the house. And it makes sense because now that we have a new baby at home, my stepfather seems to be traveling more, and there is tension in the house when he returns. Now my sisters and I secretly hope that he'll stay away to avoid their fighting. When he returns, he goes straight to the liquor cabinet and makes himself a scotch on the rocks and then turns on the stereo. He sweeps his baby daughter in his arms and dances with her to Frank Sinatra or Burt Bacharach as we look on. She clings to his neck and when he twirls in circles faster and faster she begins to laugh. I look at my mother, arms crossed against her chest, and watch her face slowly soften even in apprehension. How can this man, dancing gleefully with his daughter, cause so much pain?

## MY PAPA'S WALTZ
### Theodore Roethke (1908–1963)

The whiskey on your breath
Could make a small boy dizzy;
But I hung on like death:
Such waltzing was not easy.

We romped until the pans
Slid from the kitchen shelf;
My mother's countenance
Could not unfrown itself.

The hand that held my wrist
Was battered on one knuckle;

At every step you missed
My right ear scraped a buckle.

You beat time on my head
With a palm caked hard by dirt,
Then waltzed me off to bed
Still clinging to your shirt.

———

When I discover Theodore Roethke's poem "My Papa's Waltz" I am reminded of those moments in our house with my stepfather. Did I love this man? I think in my child's soul I did. Was he mine to have? I'm not sure. This poem captures all that I felt and sensed of him. Told from the perspective of a son waltzing with his father, the poem portrays a father's love and rage, and a son's need to hold on at all costs. Though its cadences and use of rhyme mimic the quality of a playful waltz, the poem's undertones foretell fear and danger.

The poem takes as its subject the relationship between a father and a son, and even in absence, the lifelong command a father wields. A poem begins by setting a mood so that "men can experience other people's experience," Roethke said. In spite of its misleading title, the mood of "My Papa's Waltz" is ominous and foreboding: the contrast of waltzing with its happy associations against the dangers of whiskey, of a hand "battered on one knuckle," pans leaving the shelf as the dance intensifies and the poem sashays down the page.

# DEPRESSION

## POPPIES IN OCTOBER
### Sylvia Plath

Three years after our baby sister is born, my mother's failing marriage becomes irreparable after the revelation that my stepfather has been unfaithful. They eventually divorce. I am thirteen. An ethereal, powerful presence moves into our house, consuming lightness and joy. Later I learn its name: depression. Its symptoms of lethargy and despondency overtake my mother's body and mind. Once it penetrates the atmosphere, it becomes contagious. Ennui hunkers inside me like a weight if I stay too long at home.

In the late sixties there is no language to talk about this form of melancholy, where one can barely function or get out of bed. There are times when I want to shake my mother out of her depression. Bearing witness provides its own strange strength. I know I cannot fall too. My mother needs me. When my mother is in this state, my sisters and I trade off looking after the baby. We take her for walks in her stroller or to the playground. Fix her a bowl of soup and sandwich for lunch. Watch her fill her coloring books. My mother says our baby sister has four mothers.

I sit at the edge of my mother's bed and will her to get up. Sometimes her body is limp as a rag doll. Other times she has crushing migraines and can't lift her head or let any light creep into her room. Melancholy trails her. For years, it seems, she falls in and out of this state where the lifeblood and will are seemingly washed out of her. Why can't she be like the other mothers of my friends in the neighborhood who are busy and happy when I go over to one of their houses for lunch during our break from school? Lisa's mother makes us peanut butter and mayonnaise sandwiches that make me gag on the first bite, but I get used to the strange taste. It's only lunchtime but she's in the kitchen cutting up vegetables for a roast she's planning to make for dinner. I don't like to think about my own mother, most likely back in bed now that we are off to school, with the blinds pulled down to block out the light.

In spite of everything, she does her best to be a good mother. She finds the finest Montessori school for her youngest daughter and makes friends with the new mothers. Even though we are Jewish and light the menorah on Hanukkah, once my mother married our Irish Catholic stepfather, we celebrated Christmas. A freshly cut pine tree nearly as tall as our ceiling filled our living room and along with it, the rituals of stringing popcorn and cranberries, hanging shiny red and green bulbs and ornaments, and anointing the treetop with a gold star or a white angel. Even though a part of me feels it's wrong to celebrate a Christian holiday, I like coming down the stairs on Christmas morning to be greeted by fattened stockings and a room full of wrapped presents. But once my mother's marriage begins to sour, I can't help but think that we are being punished for my mother marrying outside the faith.

Nevertheless, the Christmas tradition of giving gifts lingers on, as if my mother doesn't want to disappoint us. For Christmas, my mother saves money all year, sometimes going into debt, to buy us all presents she meticulously wraps with cutouts from magazines. When we are sick, she makes us tomato and butter sandwiches. Slowly she finds her footing again, a single woman in a world made of couples, but it's as if the black cloud of depression lives just outside our door waiting to consume us; we do everything to keep it at bay. I don't quite understand why my mother can't snap herself out of it, and I'm angry that she can't; but I also know that when she falls into this state, it's as if she's been snatched away from us and what has overtaken her is beyond our control, as if she's living in a foreign country, and yet we all live in the same house. "Why can't you make yourself happy?" my baby sister asks.

## POPPIES IN OCTOBER
### Sylvia Plath (1932–1963)

Even the sun-clouds this morning cannot manage
    such skirts.
Nor the woman in the ambulance
Whose red heart blooms through her coat so
    astoundingly—

A gift, a love gift
Utterly unasked for
By a sky

Palely and flamily
Igniting its carbon monoxides, by eyes
Dulled to a halt under bowlers.

O my God, what am I
That these late mouths should cry open
In a forest of frost, in a dawn of cornflowers.

———

I don't remember when I first discovered the poetry of Sylvia Plath. My first encounter with Plath's work might have been reading her popular novel, *The Bell Jar*—a touchstone for many introspective girls about a breakdown and recovery—when I was in high school. I am still amazed at the way in which it captures the inner state of a young woman struggling with her own ambitions and desires in the 1950s. It seems to ask whether it is possible to be a great writer and a kind, good person. I wonder if men think this way. I discover Plath's poetry later, in college. It employs powerful images like "tulips that open and close," mythological figures like Medusa, mirrors, faces, fetuses, images that evoke inner states and capture powerful feelings and unspoken emotions. "Poppies in October" articulates the wash of blackness that inhabits an individual and distorts her worldview. Plath's poems, in spite of their darkness, offer strange comfort and companionship. She has an eye that, even in despair, searches for beauty, like the bright image of red poppies in the stalls at the greengrocer on a dark day in October.

The critic Helen Vendler describes "Poppies in October"

as faultless, a "binocular vision of life and death." It conjures the mind in a melancholic state. "Oh my God, / what am I?" she asks, aware that depression has altered her. Under an October "sun-cloud" sky, an ambulance passes by carrying a bleeding woman "whose red heart blooms through her coat so astoundingly." Passersby "are dulled to a halt" witnessing the incident. The imagery is reminiscent of suicide, the carbon monoxide in the flowers, the bleeding woman, the flowers crying open. "Even the sun-clouds cannot manage such skirts," she writes of the petals of the poppies, an image so beautiful and womanly that it obliterates all else and lifts the speaker momentarily out of her despair. "It is to the ravishing beauty of the flowers the poet responds to first; . . . the ambulance seems forgotten as the senses carry Plath in gratitude for the unexpected beauty of the flowers so late in the year; they are . . . 'a love gift,'" writes Helen Vendler. "They take the poet outside her desperate melancholy state, the chill of death momentarily warded off." As Vendler affirms of Plath, "death was always before her eyes." But I wonder, is it death, or more the fear of living in a depressive state without the ability to make it lift?

# ENVY

## SONNET 29: "WHEN, IN DISGRACE WITH FORTUNE AND MEN'S EYES"
William Shakespeare

## CONFESSION
Louise Glück

I feel its burn when I look at my older sister and long for her pure white skin dotted with light freckles and the way a trail of boys comes to our house seeking her attention. I experience it when I watch sister number three consume the same plate of French fries and hamburgers I ate and not gain a pound. My sisters and I go to my cousins' house before Hebrew school. When we arrive, my aunt is in the kitchen making breakfast. Our two girl cousins are seated around the kitchen table spreading toast with an orange coat of Cheez Whiz, while their older brothers shoot baskets with my uncle in the driveway. Our house is messy and disorganized. I'm ashamed of the frayed and faded slipcovers on the furniture in our living room. Our sagging roof and clapboard frame in need of a fresh coat of paint. In my cousin's house, everything is brand new and touched by the hand of an orderly and ordinary existence. But it is more than the superficial; there is an aura of lightheartedness and well-being in their home. I wish my mother would pull out of her melancholy state and make breakfast for us every morning, but wishing it won't will her dark mood away.

I feel it when at school. I wish for one friend's long straight mane of hair and another's easy social grace. Why am I so locked inside myself? I do not expect that anyone will ever be envious of me.

## SONNET 29: "WHEN, IN DISGRACE WITH FORTUNE AND MEN'S EYES"
### William Shakespeare (1564–1616)

When, in disgrace with fortune and men's eyes
I all alone beweep my outcast state,
And trouble deaf heaven with my bootless cries,
And look upon myself and curse my fate,
Wishing me like to one more rich in hope,
Featur'd like him, like him with friends possess'd,
Desiring this man's art, and that man's scope,
With what I most enjoy contented least;
Yet in these thoughts myself almost despising,
Haply I think on thee, and then my state,
(Like to the lark at break of day arising
From sullen earth) sings hymns at heaven's gate;
   For thy sweet love rememb'red such wealth brings
   That then I scorn to change my state with kings.

After school, my sisters and I waste time at the strip mall a few blocks away from our home. We stop at Campus Drug Store to buy strands of red licorice or Draeger's ice cream shop for a sugar cone. Some days we slip onto a stool at Mawby's coffee shop for a chocolate milk shake and a plate of fries and turn our stools to the big window to watch men with their briefcases unload from the rapid transit across the street, returning from their jobs downtown. Occasionally a young wife and her small children are on the platform waiting for one of them. Sometimes we wander into My Darling Daughter, an upscale clothing store. We run our hands through the piles of soft cashmere sweaters and flip through the rack of mini dresses. Inside the store, everything is tinged with glamour and beauty. I imagine if I owned even one item from My Darling Daughter it might brush off on me too. Sometimes we dare each other to go into the dressing room to try on a sweater or dress just for the thrill of it.

One Saturday I go shopping with my friends. I have saved up enough money from babysitting, but with so many choices, it's hard to decide which sweater to buy. Finally, I decide on a pale-pink angora. When I try it on, I feel as if I have been transformed from an ordinary girl into someone special. All the way home as I hold the shopping bag with the My Darling Daughter logo embossed on it, my new sweater neatly folded between sheets of light blue tissue paper, I carry that feeling with me. But once I say goodbye to my friends, and open the door to my house, my mood turns. I think about my sisters and feel first a prickle of superiority and then quickly its underside, shame. It's complicated. If I wear my new sweater it will be like throwing it in the face of my sisters. I don't want to feel the sting of envy or scorn. And sharing it will make it less important. Instead I keep it hidden and unworn in my drawer, like a talisman.

## CONFESSION

### Louise Glück (1943–)

To say I'm without fear—
it wouldn't be true.
I'm afraid of sickness, humiliation.
Like anyone, I have my dreams.
But I've learned to hide them,
to protect myself
from fulfillment: all happiness
attracts the Fates' anger.
They are sisters, savages—
in the end they have
no emotion but envy.

———

When my son is in seventh or eighth grade he is asked to choose a Shakespeare sonnet, memorize it, and share it with his class. He chooses Sonnet 29. A Shakespearean sonnet is a fourteen-line poem in iambic pentameter. It traditionally ends with a couplet that leads to a resolution of the poem's theme or argument. Listening for the rhyme can, on the first or second reading, obscure the meaning, but it also makes a sonnet an easier poetic form to memorize. In Shakespeare's hand, the sonnets have a symmetrical beauty and are an expression of an inner argument, a way of thinking. Ostensibly about courtly romance, the sonnets were formally published in 1609 and there are 154 all together. Sonnets 1–126 address a young man and the rest a woman and chart the narrative of a love affair. How can a poem written in the seventeenth century still feel present? Perhaps it is because though time progresses, our inner emotions remain constant. As I listen to my son recite the sonnet, I remember the early years of my life when I wished for a more stable home, for my mother's happiness, for another girl's "art" and "scope," and can recall the horrible sting of my envy. "Confession" by Louise Glück, a short free-verse poem of eleven lines, turns that wish on its head by documenting the flipside: What it felt like to be the object of another's envy.

"Confession" in its short lines packs an emotional wallop. Glück, an American poet, is known for her searing poems about family dynamics and her skillful, taut, and precise use of language. "The Confession" expresses the subversive and uncomfortable feeling of being the object of envy. It explains the reason I kept my new sweater hidden in a drawer.

Both Sonnet 29 and "Confession," written centuries apart, invoke in the reader a sense of identification. Are the poems sprung from personal experience? Or an attempt to achieve universality? Or a combination of both? In answer to whether a poem is born from personal experience Louise Glück has said: "In saying to write, you're going to write that which most concerns you, which most quickens your mind, and then to turn those subjects over with as resourceful and complex a touch as possible. I am endlessly irritated by the reading of my poems as autobiography. I draw on the materials my life has given me, but what interests me isn't that they happen to me, what interests me is that they seem, as I look around, paradigmatic. We're all born mortal. We have to contend with the idea of mortality. We all, at some point, love, with the risks involved, the vulnerabilities involved, the disappointments and great thrills of passion. This is common human experience, so what you use is the self as a laboratory, in which to practice, master, what seem to you central human dilemmas."

# SEXUALITY

## THE SISTERS OF SEXUAL TREASURE
Sharon Olds

My best friend and I carouse around our neighborhood in her father's Cadillac, dubbed the "cruise mobile." We are fifteen. My friend's mother had a nervous breakdown when we were in elementary school and never fully recovered. My own mother is in a fragile state. We long to escape the constricting quiet and ennui in our homes. We stop for gas at a Sohio filling station. Two boys, older, maybe eighteen or nineteen, are in a blue Corvette across the pump from ours, and we notice, the way teenagers do, that they are looking. They're different from the boys who live in our neighborhood, less clean-cut and preppy, and maybe that's what attracts us. When one gets out of the car, I notice a bandana in the back pocket of his jeans, and when he leans over the car to push the nozzle into the gas tank, a sliver of white skin between where his jeans and T-shirt meet. He is tall and muscular. Of the two, he is the one I like. Maybe because in the dark of the night, in the restless boredom of our lives, any boy different from the pack we run with will do. Maybe all we want in that moment is not to care at all. It takes up too much energy to care.

My friend is bolder. She steps out of the car and lights up a cigarette. The other boy gets out of the car and begins to talk to her and then I get out too and the driver pumping the gas comes over, lifts his chin, and says, "Hey." We banter back and forth and then we are in their car, leaving my girl-friend's father's car in the gas station parking lot, heading to the 7-Eleven for beer. The night is suddenly dangerous, alive with possibility. The air outside the open window feels different—crisper, with an edge. I observe the driver next to me, watch his hand reach for the gearshift, the way his cheeks are sunken in, the muscle in his arm as he leans his elbow out the open window. We find a secluded spot to park underneath one of the weeping willow trees facing the duck pond and pop open our beer cans, everything quiet for a moment save the sound of the air as it escapes. The beer tastes cold and harsh and later hot as it slides down my throat. My friend is in the backseat with one boy and I am in the front with the one I like. The driver slides a cassette into the chamber of his car's tape deck and we listen to "Stairway to Heaven," "The Joker," and "Free Bird" and time disappears. Who knows or remembers what we talked about. I don't even remember their names. All we want is the boys' lips on ours, tasting like warm sour beer, and their rough hands on our hot skin. It isn't until later that night, under the nubby covers in my bed, watching the shadows of the oak tree make strange shapes on my wall, replaying the night in my mind, that it occurs to me that we might have put ourselves in danger.

## THE SISTERS OF SEXUAL TREASURE
Sharon Olds (1942–)

As soon as my sister and I got out of our
mother's house, all we wanted to
do was fuck, obliterate
her tiny sparrow body and narrow
grasshopper legs. The men's bodies
were like our father's body! The massive
hocks, flanks, thighs, elegant
knees, long tapered calves—
we could have him there, the steep
forbidden
buttocks, backs of the knees, the cock
in our mouth, ah the cock in our mouth.
      Like explorers who,
discover a lost city, we went,
nuts with joy, undressed the men,
slowly and carefully, as if
uncovering buried artifacts that
proved our theory of the lost culture:
that if Mother said it wasn't there,
it was there.

———

This unrepressed, fiery, erotic poem captures the subversive
pleasure of becoming an independent, sexual being. Two
teenage sisters discover the power of seduction and the plea-

sures of having sex and, in doing so, they obliterate the constraints and oppression of their mother and her expectations. This is a poem of liberation and the sexual act as release. When asked in an interview why she writes poems, Sharon Olds said, "You know when you have something that you long to say to someone, and you could never say it to them, to their face? Then here's a place where you could speak." Indeed, "The Sisters of Sexual Treasure" represents what is sayable perhaps only in poetry. It allows us to think about taboo emotions by pushing the envelope. Does Olds mean literally that she wants to sleep with her father? Or is she saying that a young girl's sexuality is at some level tied up with the father? The father in the poem becomes archetypal. He is all of our fathers. The daughters must prove their existence or their right to exist as separate beings from their mother by doing something they think she would disapprove of. The poem tells a classic story of teenage and adolescent rebellion, but what dwells underneath is complex and mysterious. When I discover "The Sisters of Sexual Treasure," it brings back the night in that Corvette with those boys we never saw again, and all the other nights in the dark cars, movie theaters, and dim basements of my teenage years.

# ESCAPE

## SYMPATHY
Paul Laurence Dunbar

In the early 1970s, the Vietnam War and America's involvement in it are in full throttle. When the Kent State shootings happen an hour away from Cleveland, I am a teenager and my mother is in her late thirties. My mother is single again. The world is changing, but we seem to be living in our own little stagnant capsule, where everything depends upon the illusion of well-being. I feel a revolution happening inside me too, but at the time I don't know what it means. It is a growing impatience and hostility toward my mother and her dependence on men. Now that she's divorced, she's ready to start dating again, but this time there is desperation in the enterprise.

It begins sometimes a week before, when she picks us up from school in her yellow Comet and makes a quick detour to May Company or Higbee's department store before taking us home. By the time she explores the sales racks of dresses, tries on countless pairs of high heels, stops at the make-up counter to sample the vast array of lipsticks, eye shadows, and mascaras, searching for the perfect combination of outfit and accessories, my sisters and I are exhausted and impatient, our stomachs growling. Besides, we have homework to do, tests to study for, plays to rehearse. And there is a war raging in another country, killing people; there are antiwar protests, black-power uprisings, and feminist movements. Even where I go to school a rebellion has begun. Students are experimenting with LSD and other drugs and sit in class stoned out of their minds. When I leave school, I catch whiffs of marijuana smoke in the air. The world is changing, but inside my home everything is stagnant. Why can't my mother wake up? When she's in this state it is as if the world has stopped outside our door. We have witnessed, before my mother remarried, a string of men come into our home to pick her up. And at the end of the night we've watched her return disillusioned. None of them seems worthy of her care and attention. Watching her looking into the cosmetic mirror, making that face that isn't her face, I feel trapped. Desperate to escape my mother's fate.

I no longer want to be pigeonholed, to be the pitied daughter of a desperate widow and divorcée with few options. I fear if I can't escape, I'll wind up like my mother and always wear the shameful badge of my upbringing. I work at a bakery counter after school, then later waitress and babysit, saving every cent I can for college. All I want is to be set free.


### SYMPATHY
Paul Laurence Dunbar (1872–1906)


I know what the caged bird feels, alas!
    When the sun is bright on the upland slopes;

When the wind stirs soft through the springing grass,
And the river flows like a stream of glass;
   When the first bird sings and the first bud opes,
And the faint perfume from its chalice steals—
I know what the caged bird feels!

I know why the caged bird beats his wing
   Till its blood is red on the cruel bars;
For he must fly back to his perch and cling
When he fain would be on the bough a-swing;
   And a pain still throbs in the old, old scars
And they pulse again with a keener sting—
I know why he beats his wing!

I know why the caged bird sings, ah me,
   When his wing is bruised and his bosom sore,—
When he beats his bars and he would be free;
It is not a carol of joy or glee,
   But a prayer that he sends from his heart's deep core,
But a plea, that upward to Heaven he flings—
I know why the caged bird sings!

———

Paul Laurence Dunbar, born in Dayton, Ohio, was one of the first African American poets to be known during his lifetime for verse written in black dialect. His parents' stories of their experiences as slaves living on a plantation in pre-emancipation Kentucky informed and influenced his writing. The only African American in his high school class, he was elected class president and read a poem at his high school graduation. He edited the school newspaper and the *Dayton Tattler*, a paper that was published for the African American community of West Dayton. He did not have the financial means to attend college. Instead, he attempted to find employment at a Dayton newspaper and as a legal clerk, but because of his skin color was refused. He later took a job as an elevator operator. He eventually moved to Chicago and befriended Frederick Douglas, who helped him secure a job as a clerk and invited him to read his poetry. The speaker in "Sympathy" empathizes with the bird locked in its cage, unable to explore the outside world. It no doubt reflects the poet's history, the son of former slaves, and of being confined by its legacy, enduring a pain that "still throbs in the old, old scars." But a reader can enter the poem with his or her own experience. For a young girl, it might exemplify the experience of being trapped by her parenthood, her surroundings, or by living in the wake of patriarchy. It resounds with the desire to be let loose, free, though it is not "a carol of joy and glee," because the bird's former suffering cannot be denied.

Maya Angelou drew inspiration from this poem and took a portion of it for the title of her acclaimed and widely read autobiographical novel *I Know Why the Caged Bird Sings,* a classic coming-of-age narrative about enduring bigotry and trauma in the South.

# FIRST LOVE

## BRIGHT STAR
John Keats

## A BLESSING
James Wright

I first witness the drama of improbable and quixotic attraction in sentimental movies like *Love Story*, which we view one wintry Sunday at the Vogue movie theater in the shopping mall, three sisters crying into our coat sleeves at the sad ending, and also in novels like Emily Brontë's *Wuthering Heights* or Charlotte Brontë's *Jane Eyre*. "Nothing ever becomes real till it is experienced – Even a Proverb is no proverb to you till your Life has illustrated it," John Keats, the Romantic poet, wrote in a now-famous letter to his brother and sister, "The Vale of Soul Making."

It happens when I am a senior in high school. I am at a party and in through the door he walks, wearing jeans and a wool pullover sweater, with brown thin hair tied back in a ponytail, dark hazel eyes, and chiseled cheekbones. Seeing the way he looks at me across the room, blood rushes through my veins, and I feel the way I do when sun scorches my face. His family has a big house in the country. They own two dogs, several cats, and on their properties is a barn with three horses. In addition, his father owns race horses he boards at the local harness-racing track. He tells me that he wants to become a vet and then later he changes his mind and aspires to be a harness-racing driver. When I am off my shift at the coffee shop where I wait tables, he comes by and picks me up in his blue jeep with its plastic windows, flapped open, rattling in the wind, and we spend afternoons walking through the woods near his home or trailing a creek and weekends at the racetrack where he has a job as a groom. Summer nights, after the races, I sometimes sleep with him in the track's dark tack room on a thin cot, the floors and walls cement, smelling like horse hair, but I don't care. When I go away to college my first year, I feel as if I've forgotten something. He is at loose ends, taking time off from college and still working at the track back home where he cleans stalls, grooms, and hand walks the horses hoping for a shot at becoming a driver. There is one black pay phone in the hall of our dorm and every time it rings my heart jumps, hoping it's him. One day, after I've almost gotten used to his absence, as if it's become its own muscle, and I've become strangely attracted to another student in my philosophy class—he's analytical and slightly full of himself, but nevertheless we take long walks together engaging in philosophical discussions about the texts we are reading—he surprises me and drives from Cleveland to Vermont and knocks on my dorm room door. My body comes alive like a Christmas tree all lit up. We drive through the snowy small towns in Vermont, stopping for a lunch of grilled cheese, tomato, and sprout sandwiches in a health-food store that smells of grains and vitamins. We spend the night freezing under a thin duvet in a cheap bed-and-breakfast. In the morning, freshly baked muffins and coffee await us as we walk down the creaky stairs before making the journey back to campus. In the car, he talks about us getting a little house together in Vermont with a barn and horses he could train after I graduate and growing our own vegetables and living off the land, the simple life, but the closer we get to the college where I will soon return to my dorm room and classes and he'll begin the long trek back to Cleveland, something shifts. I notice things about him I hadn't seen before. I can't share with him my growing interest in ideas and books. Around him I'm almost mute. His hair is too long and stringy. Dirt from the track is still in his nails, and he seems without ambition, whereas my mind's been turned on by the books I've been reading for my classes, and suddenly I can't contain all my ideas and wants; but still there is this attraction between us. I wish for time to stop so that nothing between us will alter, but our individual aspirations draw us further apart.

Nevertheless, for a decade, not a day goes by when I do not think about him or wish things could be different. I wonder, why do we love who we love? Why does love die? There is a fierce irrational attachment between us. I can't stand to think of him upset or hurt, and the thought of him with someone else is unbearable, even though when we are together it doesn't feel right and within days, sometimes weeks, together we break up. Just when I believe I'm over him, he shows up again unannounced, and it begins all over again. In this romantic sonnet the poet longs for the state of bliss to remain and never change.

## BRIGHT STAR
### John Keats (1795–1821)

Bright star, would I were steadfast as thou art—
  Not in lone splendor hung aloft the night
And watching, with eternal lids apart,
  Like nature's patient, sleepless Eremite,
The moving waters at their priestlike task
  Of pure ablution round earth's human shores,
Or gazing on the new soft fallen mask
  Of snow upon the mountains and the moors—
No—yet still steadfast, still unchangeable,
  Pillowed upon my fair love's ripening breast,
To feel forever its soft fall and swell,
  Awake forever in a sweet unrest,
Still, still to hear her tender-taken breath,
  And so live ever—or else swoon to death.

———

The poet John Keats died in 1821, just twenty-five years old and largely unknown. Years after his death, his genius was belatedly recognized and he is now considered among the greatest English poets. "I have loved the principle of beauty in all things," he wrote, and its guiding light informs his poetry. In 1818, as a struggling young poet, he fell in love with Fanny Brawne. She is the "bright star" of this poem.

Keats and Fanny first met in the midst of personal upheaval. Keat's youngest brother, Tom, was ill with tuberculosis; it had already killed their mother, and would eventually claim Tom and later Keats himself. It was the autumn of 1818. Keats had recently returned from a walking tour of Scotland with his friend Charles Brown. Brown had rented out his half of the double house called Wentworth Place to the Brawne family. When he returned, the Brawnes moved to Elm Cottage, a brief walk away. But while they had lived at Wentworth Place, they had become close friends with Brown's neighbors, the Dilke family, also friends of Keats's. When the Brawne family finally met the young poet, the romance between Keats and Fanny ignited.

In "Bright Star," the poet addresses the "bright" star, Polaris, eternally steadfast in the sky. Like the star, forever watching over earth, the poet wants to experience for eternity the "soft swell" of his lover's breast "and to wake forever in sweet unrest." Of course, the impossibility of this conceit is belied by the tone's melancholic state and our knowledge of his impending death. Keats died far too young—awareness of his own mortality reverberates in each wistful line—and this poem captures that romantic spirit not yet tempered by the wages of time, or altered by experience or the unbridgeable chasm of difference.

The summer before I go to college, in between our summer jobs, we hang out in the barn. The world has grown small. It seems no larger than the four walls of the barn that is home to the three beautiful mares his family owns, and to the sounds of their neighing, their bodies as they shift restlessly in their stalls, and the simple sensation of holding my boyfriend's hand, feeling the thick callouses formed from his work in the stalls. For a time my mother, my sisters, the morning headlines about how many have been killed in Vietnam, the riots and protests, what I've come to see as the superficial values of living in the suburbs that rage in my mind, my fears and worries about who I will be or become vanish and are replaced by an absurd sort of soliloquy that is playing in my head where everything has come to revolve around our togetherness.

I have never been horseback riding but being in this newly transfixed state of mind, I agree to try it. He saddles the horses and tells me we will follow an easy trail and go slow. He helps boost me into the saddle, takes the horse's bit, and walks me around the corral where the horses graze, until I get the feel of it. *Grip your thighs against his sides. Hold the reins loosely in your hands; if the horse senses your fear he will react to it.* My heart is beating crazily. I imagine it leaping out of my chest but I also experience this strange and surreal sense of safety as I watch him guide my horse. He lets go of the bit and I am on my own now, my body rising to the horse's gait, the breeze blowing back my hair. My mind is in free float. It is almost like I am disappearing. Then he straddles his own horse and opens the gate and slowly, on our horses, mine following his, we are on a trail through the trees. At first it is exhilarating. I can sense the light brush of leaves dust my shirt as we brush past. Then the horse begins to gallop and my heart races with its pace and suddenly the trail broadens into an open space and my horse takes off and

I am thrown to the ground. Everything happens so quickly, and for a minute, I lose consciousness and when I open my eyes he is standing over me and telling me not to move. The horse's back leg is standing on a piece of my waist-length hair and if I move an inch I am liable to get kicked in the face. I look into his eyes as he gently coaxes the horse slowly away. Then he holds out his hand and reaches for me and I see in his eyes his own terror of what might have happened and suddenly I realize everything in my being has become dependent upon him and the sensation is more frightening than when the horse had me pinned to the ground. When I read this poem for the first time I am reminded of my first encounter with horses and how love and attachment blossomed that summer before my first year of college.

## A BLESSING
### James Wright (1927–1980)

Just off the highway to Rochester, Minnesota,
Twilight bounds softly forth on the grass.
And the eyes of those two Indian ponies
Darken with kindness.
They have come gladly out of the willows
To welcome my friend and me.
We step over the barbed wire into the pasture
Where they have been grazing all day, alone.
They ripple tensely, they can hardly contain their happiness
That we have come.
They bow shyly as wet swans. They love each other.

There is no loneliness like theirs.
At home once more,
They begin munching the young tufts of spring in the darkness.
I would like to hold the slenderer one in my arms,
For she has walked over to me
And nuzzled my left hand.
She is black and white,
Her mane falls wild on her forehead,
And the light breeze moves me to caress her long ear
That is delicate as the skin over a girl's wrist.
Suddenly I realize
That if I stepped out of my body I would break
Into blossom.

————

This poem shimmies down the page, one line after the other, the lines breaking as thought might break. The poem tells the narrator's story of turning off the road and witnessing two ponies coming out of the field to welcome him and his friend. They step over the fence to greet the two ponies. They can "hardly contain their happiness," upon seeing them. "They love each other. / There is no loneliness like theirs," the narrator tells us, suggesting that implicit in love is loneliness. Witnessing the two ponies in love is internalized, and in describing the sensation, the narrator expresses the idea that if he stepped out of his body, he would "break into blossom." In "A Blessing," love—whether platonic or romantic—is a form of "blossoming," the same as the blossoming of a flower or a tree, and reading the poem fills me with the wonder of this phenomenon. Is this a love poem or a nature poem? No matter. A love poem can be disguised within a nature poem.

Of writing, Wright said in an interview, "Sometimes there is a force of life like the spring which mysteriously takes shape without your even having asked it to take shape, and this is frightening, it is terribly frightening. It has happened maybe a few times to me—times when I've been able to get the poem finished in almost nothing flat. . . . A poem called "Father," a poem called "A Blessing." Where did they come from? If you were to ask me that question, I would have to say, how should I know? Being a poet sometimes puts you at the mercy of life, and life is not always merciful."

# MOTHERS

## MY MOTHER'S FEET
### Stanley Plumly

Flipping through the college catalogs in the guidance counselor's office, I come across a small college, Windham, embedded in the snowy hills of Vermont and feel an affinity. It is cold and snowy in the winter and there is something magical and austere about the way in which the collection of white buildings is nestled in the hills. I fall in love immediately, and after receiving a small scholarship and a good financial-aid package, I make my decision to attend. I'm afraid to leave especially my little sister alone with my mother out of fear of my mother's dark moods, but I have no choice. If I don't go to college I fear I'll end up like her, without enough resources to be independent. The plan is that my mother and a close friend will drive me to the campus in Putney, Vermont. My eight-year-old sister will come too. My mother and her friend love to go to flea markets and antiquing, and after they drop me off, they plan to have a holiday of their own, stopping in small towns to antique along the way. All summer they carefully plan the road trip but the night before we are to leave, my trunk already packed to the brim with my jeans and sweaters, my mother becomes ill—pneumonia—and can't take me.

I book a flight to New York, where I will change planes and take a smaller plane to Burlington, Vermont. But once I arrive in New York, the flight to Burlington is canceled. Unsure of what to do, alone for the first time in a strange airport in a strange city, I panic. I call my mother, and hearing the fear in my voice, she uncharacteristically lashes out at me. *How will you manage in college, if you can't manage this?* she says, or something like it, her voice cracks and she begins to cry into the phone and I think this is the first time my mother will be without me and I without her and it is all terrible. I wonder if my leaving has made her sick. I hang up the phone, and once I return the receiver to its holder, I listen to my coins falling down inside the pay phone's deep throat into the well. I tell myself I have to be strong and pull myself together. This is probably the first day I grow up. I go to the airline counter and book a flight for the next morning and wander into one of the kiosks and wretchedly spend five or six dollars on a fat paperback edition of *Tess of the D'Urbervilles,* for then I did not like to part with my hard-earned money. I go to the gate and sit down with my book and read until the morning, wondering if the boy I've left back home is my Angel, like the character in the novel. Nothing is as terrifying to me as that day and night alone in an unknown airport in New York and when I finally land in Burlington and take a cab to the small college in the hills, I recognize I am at a turning point. I step out of the cab and breathe in the fresh, cool Vermont air that smells like pinecones. The years of high school when I feared I'd be stuck in Cleveland forever are finally over. I push back my hair, take a peppermint Life Saver from my pocket and slip it into my mouth, inhale a deep breath to calm my nerves and walk through the college arches to begin my life. In spite of the fact that, due to my late arrival, my new roommate, who has long black hair and is wearing dark lipstick before goth has come into vogue, has already decorated her side of the wall with posters of Kiss and other metal bands, and I am more of a Neil Young and James Taylor girl, it's all good. Really good.

I enjoy being shut up in the library where I have a work-study job shelving books and organizing the card catalog, or in my dorm room reading and studying. I like listening out my dorm-room door to the chatter and occasional horseplay in the halls that reek of cigarettes and pot. I like sharing the coed bathroom with the boys on our floor and the routine of going to the cafeteria for my meals, pushing my tray along the line and deciding which item I will take, whether a plate of cottage cheese and fruit or a green salad, mashed potatoes and meatloaf, or the vegetarian lasagna. I like meeting new and more sophisticated friends from Los Angeles and New York City, the spontaneous dorm parties where we all crash in one room, walks in the woods discussing politics or parsing out the meaning behind a Wallace Stevens or T. S. Eliot poem. It is the first time in my life that I am separated from my family and it is liberating. Unfortunately, the college goes bankrupt after my first year and I don't know what I'll do. I spend the summer taking a waitressing job back home, but I'm restless, bored, and unhappy. It doesn't occur to me—for a reason I can't recall—that I can consider applying or transferring to another college of my choice. Sister number three is beginning her freshman year at Ohio University in Athens, Ohio, known as Athens on the Hill. Without another plan, I decide to join her, packing up my trunk again and hoping once I arrive on campus, they will take me, and miraculously, they do. It is easy since I am an Ohio resident. And, as fate will have it, now a sophomore in college, I sign up for my first creative writing workshop and another new chapter begins.

In the classroom in Ellis Hall that held our poetry seminar, its open windows facing onto the college green, I am both excited and anxious. I've never written a serious poem before, only jottings in my diaries and notebooks. With his shock of salt-and-pepper hair and matching beard, and his gentle yet commanding voice, our professor-poet tells us to write poems about what we know and what hurts. Every week he passes out copies of our poems freshly printed on mimeographed paper—I can still recall the paper's sharp smell of metallic purple ink—and if we defy his assignment by writing poems with generic or meaningless subject matter, he tears up our poems and tosses them into the wastebasket.

I lived under the assumption that one must hide hurt and pain, that sadness and sorrow are reserved for the solitude of one's own private world. I go back to my dorm and think about what my poet-teacher has said. What I know has to do with my childhood and being born into a world of grief and loss and I have been given permission to write about it. My desk faces the window. Outside, it is snowing, an unexpected snowfall in late autumn before all the leaves have fallen and white flakes begin to fill the college green. I remember the snowy winters of my childhood, and the memories evoke a mood I want to capture. But how? Images spring forth. Sisters playing in the snow. A widow in her bed. Houseplants on a windowsill. A tall tree in the yard spreading its fatherly branches over the house. I write into that world of sadness and sorrow I experienced as a young child. Over time the verse evolves into a poem in ten small parts called "Fathers in the Snow" about a widow caring for her small children and the undercurrent of loss permeating their home. For years I've been trapped inside my own strange fear and grief, and now it is liberated into verse.

The idea that poetry should take as its subject matter the painful aspects of my existence opens a new way of thinking for me. I seem to have been waiting for it. I realize that through the artfulness of poetic form, one can trap experience and make it palpable to a reader. A poem might be about what hurts, and most illuminating, the subject might be drawn from one's own life. A poem could be both personal and communal and save a person from the dark shadow of shame. It may take as its form an address to a person, real or imagined, historical or alive today. It might be an off-kilter love letter to someone as significant as one's mother.

## MY MOTHER'S FEET
### Stanley Plumly (1939–)

How no shoe fit them,
and how she used to prop them,
having dressed for bed,
letting the fire in the coal-stove blue

and blink out, falling asleep in her chair.
How she bathed and dried them, night after night,
and rubbed their soreness like an intimacy.
How she let the fire pull her soft body through them.

She was the girl who grew just standing,
the one the picture cut at the knees.
She was the girl who seemed to be dancing
out on the lawn, after supper, alone.

I have watched her climb the militant stairs
and down again, watched the ground go out from under her.
I have seen her on the edge of chances—
she fell, when she fell, like a girl.

Someone who loved her said she walked on water.
Where there is no path nor wake. As a child
I would rise in the half-dark of the house,
from a bad dream or a noisy window,

something, almost, like snow in the air,
and wander until I could find those feet, propped
and warm as a bricklayer's hands,
every step of the way shining out of them.

———

Like Pablo Neruda's "Ode To My Socks," this poem show-
cases how anything—even a pair of feet—can be subject mat-
ter for poetry and allow for revelation. "My Mother's Feet" is

not only a love letter from a son to his mother, but also a trib-
ute to the universal "ideal" of mothers. The poem captures
that turning point in a child's life when suddenly he or she
recognizes a parent as a person with an inner life, someone
who has loved and lived outside her role as a mother. The
speaker has watched his mother "climb the militant stairs /
and down again, watched the ground go out from under
her." The poem uses the metaphor of feet to document the
many worlds his mother has inhabited. Feet are intimate.
They're mostly hidden underneath stockings, or inside slip-
pers, just as our mother's interior lives are concealed, and
when they appear in open sandals or barefoot on the cold
stairs, it feels as if we should turn our heads away, that we've
been exposed to something we aren't supposed to see.

Stanley Plumly, my poet-teacher, and the author of this
poem, was born in Barnesville, Ohio. His father worked in
the lumber trade and died of alcoholism in his fifties. Of his
father, Plumly said: "I can hardly think of a poem I've writ-
ten that at some point in its history did not implicate, or fig-
ure, my father." His mother also figures prominently as the
silent, helpless witness of her husband's self-destruction and
we hear reverberations of that witness in the tender and poi-
gnant "My Mother's Feet."

I discover this poem years later in graduate school when
I'm in my early twenties, no longer a child or a teenager, sur-
rounded by a library of books, my days filled with lectures
and the hint of opportunity, far away from my two sisters
who have also left home to pursue their education, and my
mother and youngest sister now in junior high school still liv-
ing back home in the house I grew up in. Not a day goes by

where I don't worry or think about them. With all us older sisters gone, they have formed their own unit of two. I pray my mother is in a good period. When her melancholy lifts, her life ignites with new purpose. She goes out with her friends, works part-time at a clothing store in the mall. A window opens. I see my mother separate from me, a woman with her own history, struggles, burdens. She was once the age I am now, when she first married, her life filled with promise and then everything for her had shattered. I swell with empathy and love.

# FRIENDSHIP

TAKING THE HANDS
    Robert Bly
SOMEWHERE I HAVE NEVER
TRAVELLED,GLADLY BEYOND
    E. E. Cummings

At Ohio University I hold three jobs. Twenty hours a week I log in and read submissions for the *Ohio Review*, a prominent literary magazine. On weekends I take orders and ring the cash register at a sub shop in town. And during the week I work the dish line in the university cafeteria dish room. A friend from my poetry class works the same shift. We come rushing to the dish room from class, clock in, don our white aprons, and join the full-time cafeteria workers, the men and women from Athens, Ohio, some with young families of their own to support. When the trays come down the belt, our job is to take the dishes off the trays and stack them. After our shift, every table wiped and polished, floors glittering, the last of the student-stragglers having left, my friend and I sit in the empty cafeteria, and sip our cups of milky Lipton tea and workshop each other's nascent poems until by seven or eight the blackness of night begins to press against the windows.

My friend is blond and thin, with long bony fingers and wide brown eyes. Her smile reveals two slightly overlapping front teeth. She reads my poems and I read hers and together we form connections between the bits and pieces of interior life hidden in the poem's blank spaces, crossing out unnecessary words and phrases, moving a line here or there. Along with reading each other's poems, we discuss the poems we are studying in class and flip through our anthologies together, sharing poems we admire. While other students are attempting to solve math proofs and chemistry problems, we are studying poetic form. In the poetry workshop we discover a wide array by exploring how poems gain their power; for example, we read the work of Robert Bly for its simplicity of language; E. E. Cummings's for the way in which syntax and punctuation transform meaning; James Wright's for his narrative gifts and symbolism embedded in images of the natural world. We read Pound, Eliot, and Marianne Moore, sometimes struggling over their poems' intellectual girth and use of literary allusions. I can picture my friend's hands sitting across from me at the long linoleum cafeteria table as she holds the page of one of my poems, and then takes the pencil behind her ear and begins to mark it up. Through poetry our friendship deepens.

## TAKING THE HANDS
Robert Bly (1926–)

Taking the hands of someone you love,
You see they are delicate cages . . .
Tiny birds are singing
In the secluded prairies
And in the deep valleys of the hand.

———

My penciled marks at the bottom of this poem in my battered copy of *Silence in the Snowy Fields* I purchase at the college bookstore read:

> Bly uses one clear metaphor in order to arrest a few moments of emotional life. The hands of someone you love become delicate cages where birds are singing. Bly celebrates the small idea of a hand holding the wonders of nature to comment on love and friendship. Poetry is an attempt to find, discover something and embody it in the cage of a poem. Bly has embodied love in the delicate cages of the hand. The entire poem is a metaphor.

This poem is an example of the deep image, a literary term invented by poets Robert Kelly and Jerome Rothenberg and later employed by Robert Bly, James Wright, and other poets of their generation to describe and define aspects of their own poetics. It is a poetic technique that uses concrete language and expressions (in this poem, the image of a hand) to express poetic meaning. Through the delicate artfulness of this small five-line poem, the metaphysical inner connections between the spiritual world and the physical world that occur when we hold someone's hands are made visible.

Influenced by European poets like Lorca and Neruda and as a reaction against the scholarly poetry of Pound and Eliot, Robert Bly stated that he was "interested in the connection between poetry and simplicity. . . . The fundamental world of poetry is an inward world. We approach it through solitude." Now, whenever I reach for someone's hand, or someone reaches for mine, I think of Bly's poem and the mysteries held within it, and those days in the cafeteria in the early evening just before dusk, my friend across from me, her brow wrinkling in thought and concentration, as the two of us analyze lines of poetry typed on thin sheets of white, onion-skin paper, as intensely as if we were surgeons operating on a patient.

Bly's "Taking the Hands" reminds me of this delicate love poem by E. E. Cummings, where a pair of hands figure as a closing image.

## SOMEWHERE I HAVE NEVER TRAVELLED,GLADLY BEYOND
### E. E. Cummings (1894–1962)

somewhere i have never travelled,gladly beyond
any experience,your eyes have their silence:
in your most frail gesture are things which enclose me,
or which i cannot touch because they are too near

your slightest look easily will unclose me
though i have closed myself as fingers,
you open always petal by petal myself as Spring opens
(touching skilfully,mysteriously)her first rose

or if your wish be to close me,i and
my life will shut very beautifully,suddenly,
as when the heart of this flower imagines
the snow carefully everywhere descending;

nothing which we are to perceive in this world equals
the power of your intense fragility:whose texture
compels me with the colour of its countries,
rendering death and forever with each breathing

(i do not know what it is about you that closes
and opens;only something in me understands
the voice of your eyes is deeper than all roses)
nobody,not even the rain,has such small hands

———

How is it that one person can unlock something private
within us? Or awaken things in us we fear? How can one
person know us more intimately than any other, or even
than we know ourselves? "The voice of your eyes is deeper
than all roses," Cummings writes, the use of the word
"voice" as a modifier for "eyes" allows the reader to experi-
ence how much the speaker of this poem "sees" into his
subject.

Cummings composed poetry as a child, writing a poem every day. He is known for his signature experimental use of poetic form, voice, and vision, sometimes employing invented words, turning nouns into verbs, and avoiding standard use of punctuation and capitalization. Yet underlying the word play, the polyphonic layering of voices, and parentheses buried within parenthesis, flows tender emotion.

# PASSION

After I graduate from the Iowa Writers' Workshop in the early 1980s, I move to New York City to embark upon what I've come to consider my true calling: becoming a poet. The city is a strange, forbidding place, so many people trapped on one island. I am overwhelmed by the smells of rotting fruit and cooked meat from the street vendors, the garbage, the way in which the city's inhabitants adopt the street as their private living room. I'm a Midwest girl; I'm used to open spaces. There are times when I begin to doubt my calling and my reasons for being here. I won't survive on poetry alone. I have to eat and figure out how to support myself. I go to Bolton's discount clothing store and buy my first suit and pair of black pumps for job interviews. The color of the pencil skirt and matching jacket I choose is cranberry, and when I look in the mirror, I feel immediately grown up. I barely recognize myself. I answer an ad in the *New York Times* for a position as an editorial assistant for a religion and philosophy editor at a university press where I'm required to take a typing test. I interview and am hired for the position. I'm glad to have a job that pays the rent, offers health benefits, and doesn't involve waiting on customers in a restaurant.

It's my first real nine-to-five job. I type letters, file correspondence, and take phone messages. I prepare manuscripts for production and occasionally read submissions and write reports about them. I'm fascinated by the various stages of how a book is made, how it arrives in the form of carefully typed manuscript pages and roughly twelve months later it becomes a book. I share a tiny, two-room apartment on West Seventy-Third, in a building where many aging ex–Zeigfield Follies actresses reside, with a poet friend and classmate from the Iowa Workshop. When I pass through the lobby on my way to work, the ladies, with their dyed blue-and-purple hair, thick make-up, and sagging skin, congregate there with their shopping carts, glancing at themselves in the mirrored wall. In Midtown the city is a teeming hive of concrete and glass. Everywhere I look, more buildings, more anonymous strangers filling subway cars and rushing in and out of offices. At night, home from the office, I retire to my room, sit at my musty, flea-market-find oak desk, turn on my Selectric typewriter, and work on poems. I flip through poetry books for inspiration and companionship. I am restless, unsure, lonely. Eight months pass and I hear about a new position at a trade house that publishes fiction and poetry and is more suited to my interests. I apply and am offered a job and eagerly accept. I like my new job, but I wonder if I've made the right choice, if I'll ever publish a book of my own, or be able to support myself in this city. Outside my window, in the street below, people dine in cafés and drink in bars, or stroll home after the theater or a concert. Sometimes it seems as if the whole city is going on without me and an unnamed desire travels through my being. Sometimes that desire is so great I can't contain it. I get dressed and go out and walk up and down Broadway just to get out of my own head. The desire is like a red coal burning inside my body.

## THE RED COAL
### Gerald Stern (1925–)

Sometimes I sit in my blue chair trying to remember
what it was like in the spring of 1950
before the burning coal entered my life.

I study my red hand under the faucet, the left one
below the grease line consisting of four feminine angels
and one crooked broken masculine one

and the right one lying on top of the white porcelain
with skin wrinkled up like a chicken's
beside the razor and the silver tap.

I didn't live in Paris for nothing and walk
with Jack Gilbert down the wide sidewalks
thinking of Hart Crane and Apollinaire

and I didn't save the picture of the two of us
moving through a crowd of stiff Frenchmen
and put it beside the one of Pound and Williams

unless I wanted to see what coals had done
to their lives too. I say it with vast affection,
wanting desperately to know what the two of them

talked about when they lived in Pennsylvania
and what they talked about at St. Elizabeth's
fifty years later, looking into the sun,

40,000 wrinkles between them,
the suffering finally taking over their lives.
I think of Gilbert all the time now, what

we said on our long walks in Pittsburgh, how
lucky we were to live in New York, how strange
his great fame was and my obscurity,

how we now carry the future with us, knowing
every small vein and every elaboration.
The coal has taken over, the red coal

is burning between us and we are at its mercy—
as if a power is finally dominating
the two of us; as if we're huddled up

watching the black smoke and the ashes;
as if knowledge is what we needed and now
we have that knowledge. Now we have that knowledge.

The tears are different—though I hate to speak
for him—the tears are what we bring back to the
darkness, what we are left with after our

own escape, what, all along, the red coal had
in store for us as we moved softly,
either whistling or singing, either listening or reasoning,

on the gray sidewalks and the green ocean;
in the cars and the kitchens and the bookstores;
in the crowded restaurants, in the empty woods and
     libraries.

———

"The Red Coal" recounts a story of two young poets, strolling
through the streets of Paris, talking about their poetic prede-
cessors, Hart Crane and Apollinaire, remembering the time
when they were young intellectuals attempting to make a life
through poetry. One poet has achieved more success than an-
other poet, but I'm not sure that's what the poem is mostly

about. It documents that burning thing inside us, whether it is a passion for poetry or art, or medicine, or law, or being a construction worker, or a chef. The burning coal is that thing we must find in life, our raison d'être, our calling.

There is another desire pulsing through me. It is a desire, as a grown woman, to meet my match and find a partner. But it seems impossible here. There is something about being in a populated city full of individuals with like-minded ambition that makes my loneness all the more palpable.

Over time I begin to create my own mental map, my preferred routes and destinations. The Italian coffee house I like to go to for iced cappuccino, the Korean greengrocer where I buy my fruit and morning bran muffins, my path through the park on a Sunday. But at the end of the day, something happens sometimes when everyone turns homeward and the neon lights of the city flicker on. Loneliness becomes its own continent. It makes me question who I am and the choices I've made. I recognize that many people my age are working in the financial world, they're lawyers and traders, or training to be doctors, or they work in advertising and fashion. When I'm not worried about how I'm going to pay my monthly rent on my meager salary, I worry about the career I've marked out. I recognize that being a poet is not a career. It is something to do in the secret hours of the early morning or late at night, in the cracks and crevices of a weekend, but it isn't enough to sustain a livelihood. I begin to wonder about my choices. After a string of unfulfilling encounters with men I meet in cafés or at poetry readings or artist residencies or parties, men who claim to be one thing and turn out to be another, who are smug or self-absorbed or nutcases or too much in love with me or not quite in love with me, I begin to lose hope. At night, I grow sentimental and nostalgic and remember my first love who absorbed so many years of my psychic and emotional attention and wonder, does he think about me too? Would I have been happier had I stayed in Cleveland?

## WHAT LIPS MY LIPS HAVE KISSED, AND WHERE, AND WHY
### Edna St. Vincent Millay (1892–1950)

What lips my lips have kissed, and where, and why,
I have forgotten, and what arms have lain
Under my head till morning; but the rain
Is full of ghosts tonight, that tap and sigh
Upon the glass and listen for reply,
And in my heart there stirs a quiet pain
For unremembered lads that not again
Will turn to me at midnight with a cry.
Thus in the winter stands the lonely tree,
Nor knows what birds have vanished one by one,
Yet knows its boughs more silent than before:
I cannot say what loves have come and gone,
I only know that summer sang in me
A little while, that in me sings no more.

———

Edna St. Vincent Millay had many love affairs. Her biographer, Nancy Milford, said of her: She smoked in public when it was against the law for women to do so, she lived in Greenwich Village during the halcyon days of that starry bohemia, she slept with men and women and wrote about it in lyrics and sonnets that blazed with wit and a sexual daring that captured the nation. This wistful sonnet was written in 1923 when Millay was thirty-one years old. The poem opens with the speaker in contemplation, alone at night, listening to the rain, remembering the ghosts of past lovers that "tap against the window." The last lines are terribly sad and beautiful, softened and consoled perhaps by memory of a love affair and the notion that at one time "summer sang in me," even though no more. I once heard that Sigmund Freud said all literature is about love and sex or was it love and death? I would venture to say that all poetry to an extent is about unrequited love, not necessarily carnal or romantic love, but yearning.

One Sunday morning I wake up early and walk on Broadway to Fairway for my breakfast: a muffin, peaches, cherries, and melon. On the streets are crates of rotted fruit and garbage in piles, waiting for pick-up. The sidewalks are dirty and in need of a scrub down. Heat rises from the subway grates and for a moment I feel faint. Up this early, all I see around me are homeless men wrapped in dirty layers of clothing and homeless women pushing shopping carts. I don't know why I am here anymore, why I am working all day in the office and coming home on nights and weekends to read submissions of debut novels and short stories, hoping to find, in sheaves of paper that pile up into a toppling tower on the floor of my two-room apartment, the living breathing soul and voice of a story that will eventually get printed and published and sell zillions of copies so I can eventually get a promotion. It is summer and I think of the green fields and parks and simple ways of living where I grew up and that I've forgone and emotion wells inside me. Maybe it's time to call it quits and go home.

## THE TROPICS IN NEW YORK
### Claude McKay (1889–1948)

Bananas ripe and green, and ginger-root,
   Cocoa in pods and alligator pears,
And tangerines and mangoes and grape fruit,
   Fit for the highest prize at parish fairs,

Set in the window, bringing memories,
   Of fruit-trees laden by low-singing rills,
And dewy dawns, and mystical blue skies
   In benediction over nun-like hills.

My eyes grew dim, and I could no more gaze;
   A wave of longing through my body swept,
And, hungry for the old, familiar ways,
   I turned aside and bowed my head and wept.

———

Claude McKay, a Jamaican poet, published his first collection of verse, *Songs of Jamaica*, when he was twenty-three. Written in Jamaican dialect, the poems trace his vision and experience of black life in his country of origin. Later, after moving to Harlem, his poetry turned to themes of social justice, race, and the lives of the working class. In this poem, the speaker, sitting by a window in a New York City apartment looking at the tropical fruit on his windowsill, longs for the tropics where he grew up. Its elegiac hues of mourning and nostalgia recalled my own mood, a girl from Cleveland, struggling to find my way in America's largest metropolis filled with inhabitants from around the globe here for the very reasons I am—to push their limits and reinvent themselves from the obscurity from which they came.

I don't want it to happen, but jadedness begins to creep in. I doubt I will ever fall in love again or find a partner to marry. My girlfriends and I meet in coffee shops and cafés and discuss the grim pickings. We sometimes go to bars or parties in hopes of meeting someone. If we go out with someone, we come home and share the encounter, wonder if he'll call again. Usually he doesn't. Or if he does, he's not the one we want. I'm grateful for my books, my deep infatuation with literature, and my poems, however nascent. I've come to see that the only thing now worth holding on to is the collection of verse accumulating on my desk and in my drawer. They don't often amount to much, but when they do I sense something alive and crackling, like the sound of stepping on twigs in the woods. In the absence of love, I cling to my work. Literature is the only thing that I can count on; it won't desert me. I can open one of the many books stacked on the floor in my room, flip through the thin pages of poetry in my Norton Anthology and call forth the passages of experience I've already known, or others I might go toward. I can find myself pulled forward and pushed back and sometimes both in one illuminating paragraph or surprising stanza.

I convince myself it is enough. I decide that I'll pursue a career in publishing and become an editor. I want to find manuscripts that boil under the skin, get under the rind. It's better than the connections I forge and then can't seem to hold on to, or the ones I invest too much in and realize they're flimsy as gauze. And it's hot in August in New York, suffocating with no air conditioning, and everyone left in the city with nowhere to go seems to have a perpetual mustache of sweat above the lip. I'm sick of hot, airless parties where I come home with smoke in my hair, nights sitting on bar stools sharing a glass of wine with my roommate because we don't have enough money to each buy a glass, where the only people we meet are struggling actors or penniless poets, or guys who work on sets ensconced in their own mini dramas. I'm sick of artists and writers, some living in cheap sublets in the East Village, others who want to move in, whose own lustful ambitions outpace their desire for intimate connection. I want a grown-up life; a family. For almost a year I saddle myself to an academic who is decent enough to pay the check when he takes me out to dinner, though when he begins to talk about one of the monographs he's working on, I find my eyes glazing over, until I discover all the while he's been pining for someone else.

# HEAT

### Denis Johnson (1949–2017)

Here in the electric dusk your naked lover
tips the glass high and the ice cubes fall against her teeth.
It's beautiful Susan, her hair sticky with gin,
Our Lady of the Wet Glass-Rings on the Album Cover,
streaming with hatred in the heat
as the record falls and the snake-band chords begin
to break like terrible news from the Rolling Stones,
and such a last light—full of spheres and zones.
August,
        you're just an erotic hallucination,
just so much feverishly produced kazoo music,
are you serious?—this large oven impersonating night,
this exhaustion mutilated to resemble passion,
the bogus moon of tenderness and magic
you hold out to each prisoner like a cup of light?

———

This poem with its sorrowful, jaded irony is born out of the frustration of being held captive by destructive illusions. It is from Denis Johnson's *Incognito Lounge*, his third book of poems, which comes out when I am in graduate school. The poems are deeply personal and depict a moment—a time, a place, a rhythm—that magically becomes equally personal for the reader. Mostly set in an apartment or in bars, the poems depict a desperate yearning—a cup of light—among the ruins.

# LEGACY

## FURY
Lucille Clifton

## DIVING INTO THE WRECK
Adrienne Rich

My maternal great-aunts Harriet and Florence never had children. Aunt Florence is a twin whose sister, Lillian, is in love with a married man from the military. When the affair ends, she suffers a psychotic break and is institutionalized until the day she dies. Aunt Florence never recovers from losing her twin to mental illness. Every Sunday the family piles into the car on an outing to the institution to see Lillian. My mother, I'm later told, is required to wait in the car while they go in to visit. Aunt Florence lives with her own mother, my great grandma Cookie, in a two-bedroom apartment. She works for May Company as a secretary, riding the rapid transit downtown to work and back. Every time we see her she opens a May company shopping bag and takes out a handful of sweaters in different sizes and colors, which she purchases on discount for us. Usually they're out of style or not quite what we like or don't fit but we pretend we love them. She's the eccentric aunt, singing us vaudeville songs she used to perform in high school to entertain us. She passes the evening reading Harlequin romance novels in the bedroom (we see them stacked up on her nightstand) with the twin beds she once shared with her twin. I am not sure if she's ever fallen in love.

My Aunt Harriet is luckier. She married a veteran from the navy, Uncle Joe with his big belly laugh who became a dentist and is a lodge brother. Every year he takes us to the circus with his lodge group. Aunt Harriet fusses over him, laughs at his jokes, and rolls her eyes when he takes it too far and she's not amused. She is the perfect housewife. There is never anything out of place in their modest apartment. She always graces the table with her good wedding china and silver when we are invited for lunch. One shelf in the living room holds the souvenirs they brought from their travels abroad, which are a source of great pride to both of them. There's an oriental fan from Japan and a clock from Sweden. Aunt Harriet's greatest misfortune is that she could not bear children. Instead, she adopts my mother after my mother's mother suddenly dies when she is nine. My mother is schooled by these women who were born in the 1920s, with their matching hats, white gloves, and stylish suits or cardigan sets they wear whenever they go out—to smile, wear lipstick, flatter and charm, and never show anyone you're suffering pain or misfortune. It is their way and my mother's legacy. "Iris, smile," they say when we trail into their home, my mother leading her flock of girls for Shabbat or brunch. They're overjoyed when my mother marries my father, a modest wedding in the rabbi's study, and heartbroken when my father dies a young death and my mother is left a widow at the age of twenty-five. "Poor, poor Iris," they say.

The conversations at the dinner table are about how my mother is faring and how we're doing in school. Uncle Joe slips us dollar bills under the table to put in our pockets, and at the end of the evening, Aunt Harriet takes my mother into her bedroom where she writes her a check. Even when times are bleak, we pretend everything is fine. Mom sometimes talks about the dates she goes on and if there is someone in particular she likes her eyes light up. But when there's a dry spell her eyes are dull as old rusted pennies. Most of my mother's friends and female relatives are married and have husbands to take care of them. When we are in their company I don't see desperation hidden underneath the layers of careful makeup in the faces of these women. They may be unhappy, but they don't have to worry about how they're going to pay the bills. I know my mother wishes her life were like theirs, but it's not and she still can't seem to accept it. Even my aunts feel as if she will be crippled if she doesn't find a new man.

After my mother's divorce from her second husband, my sisters and I try to push my mother. We urge her to take classes, find a job, and for a time she works as a receptionist, sells real estate, then works in retail, but there is a layer of fatigue and resentment underneath it all. It's as if she feels she's still entitled to the life she was meant to have, but there's no husband at home taking care of her. When I am struggling to build my own life, I worry about my mother still at home in the house I grew up in. I think of all she has sacrificed for her early dream of becoming a wife and a young mother and I wonder whether it was worth it. What might she have become if her aspirations were not confined to the norm of women of her era? What might her life have been like if she finished college before she'd gotten married, if her father and relatives urged and helped her to pursue a vocation? Though it makes no real sense, I feel guilty for her sacrifice of my being in the world. My mother loves her daughters but I know that sometimes we get on her nerves, with all our histrionics, wants, and fighting, and I sometimes wonder if she feels as if it were all a big mistake.

## fury
Lucille Clifton (1936–2010)

*for mama*

remember this.
she is standing by
the furnace.
the coals
glisten like rubies.
her hand is crying.
her hand is clutching
a sheaf of papers.
poems.
she gives them up.
they burn
jewels into jewels.
her eyes are animals.

each hank of her hair
is a serpent's obedient
wife.
she will never recover.
remember. there is nothing
you will not bear
for this woman's sake.

———

In this scalding poem, a woman's ambition is sacrificed, a handful of poems thrown into the fire. Now her eyes are fierce as animals. She is the "obedient wife" and she "will never recover." The woman has sacrificed her ambitions and in that sense she has also surrendered her dreams. At the end, the poem turns and speaks directly to the reader: "there is nothing / you will not bear / for this woman's sake." It asks us to consider the sacrifices our forbearers made and the results of those sacrifices, and what we must bear in return. Lucille Clifton once wrote: "I am not interested if anyone knows whether or not I am familiar with big words. I am interested in trying to render big ideas in a simple way. I am interested in being understood not admired."

For the rest of my mother's life, I will mourn the fact that, though she tried to find sustaining work in between the years in which my father died and she remarried and then again after she divorced, like many women of her generation, she never reconciled herself to life without a partner. Every time I come home to visit my mother, the only difference in the house I grew up in is the color of the paint on the walls, or a lamp moved from one table to another. I become more aware of how fortunate I am to be able to forge a life of independence and to secure my own livelihood. My ambition is fueled by my desire to be self-sufficient and not to rely on anyone. It is my mother's unspoken gift to her daughters.

## DIVING INTO THE WRECK
### Adrienne Rich (1950–2012)

First having read the book of myths,
and loaded the camera,
and checked the edge of the knife-blade,
I put on
the body-armor of black rubber
the absurd flippers
the grave and awkward mask.
I am having to do this
not like Cousteau with his
assiduous team
aboard the sun-flooded schooner
but here alone.

There is a ladder.
The ladder is always there

hanging innocently
close to the side of the schooner.
We know what it is for,
we who have used it.
Otherwise
it's a piece of maritime floss
some sundry equipment.

I go down.
Rung after rung and still
the oxygen immerses me
the blue light
the clear atoms
of our human air.
I go down.
My flippers cripple me,
I crawl like an insect down the ladder
and there is no one
to tell me when the ocean
will begin.

First the air is blue and then
it is bluer and then green and then
black I am blacking out and yet
my mask is powerful
it pumps my blood with power
the sea is another story
the sea is not a question of power
I have to learn alone

to turn my body without force
in the deep element.

And now: it is easy to forget
what I came for
among so many who have always
lived here
swaying their crenellated fans
between the reefs
and besides
you breathe differently down here.

I came to explore the wreck.
The words are purposes.
The words are maps.
I came to see the damage that was done
and the treasures that prevail.
I stroke the beam of my lamp
slowly along the flank
of something more permanent
than fish or weed

the thing I came for:
the wreck and not the story of the wreck
the thing itself and not the myth
the drowned face always staring
toward the sun
the evidence of damage
worn by salt and sway into this threadbare beauty
the ribs of the disaster

curving their assertion
among the tentative haunters.

This is the place.
And I am here, the mermaid whose dark hair
streams black, the merman in his armored body
We circle silently
about the wreck
We dive into the hold.
I am she: I am he

whose drowned face sleeps with open eyes
whose breasts still bear the stress
whose silver, copper, vermeil cargo lies
obscurely inside barrels
half-wedged and left to rot
we are the half-destroyed instruments
that once held to a course
the water-eaten log
the fouled compass

We are, I am, you are
by cowardice or courage
the one who find our way
back to this scene
carrying a knife, a camera
a book of myths
in which
our names do not appear.

———

My mother's generation of women who came of age in the 1950s and 1960s was the last to view their options as being largely limited to the roles of housewife and mother. The feminist movement and its trailblazers, Simone de Beauvoir, Gloria Steinem, Betty Friedan, and poets like Audre Lorde and Adrienne Rich, were changing the landscape of possibility for women. But change came slowly. My mother's generation came of age just under the radar of the women's movement and hence slipped between the cracks of those women who were still dependent on men for their survival and women who were finding their own way in the world. Bearing witness to my mother's conundrum set the stage for who I would become and the life I would lead.

"Diving into the Wreck" was written in 1973, two years before I graduate from high school, though I don't discover it until years later in college. All poems become, to a certain degree, personal to a reader. The human and the divine, sexuality, beauty, enclosure, sacrifice, freedom, discovery, all reside within this poem's wide breadth. It asks us to consider, among other things, the myths we are borne into and the myths we must challenge. It pushes against the canonical poetry that came before and writes its way into history.

The Irish poet Eavan Boland said of Adrienne Rich's work: "These poems came to the very edge of the rooms I worked in, dreamed in, listened for a child's cry in. . . . I felt that the life I lived was not the one these poems commended. It was too far from the tumult, too deep in the past. And yet these poems helped me live it. . . . Truly important poets change two things and never one without the other: the interior of the poem and external perceptions of the identity of the poet."

When I enter the workplace, it is still dominated by white men. In the literary world, white male poets are in positions of power, chairing committees, choosing poets for prizes and jobs, and all too often denying opportunities to women and people of color. Adrienne Rich wrote about the vicissitudes of injustice in pathbreaking, timeless work, without which a vast cut of present poetry would never have been written or even contemplated. Her work is eerily prescient.

The speaker in "Diving into the Wreck" is alone aboard a "sun-flooded schooner." She carefully and slowly descends into the ocean looking for a certain shipwreck. She is not a famous explorer like Cousteau with his crew and deep knowledge of the sea; she is a woman alone on the journey, wearing her wetsuit and mask and awkward flippers. She descends from the illusion of reality—the world in which she has read the "book of myths"—into the magical, enlightening reality of the ocean, where the shipwreck lies in black waters, looking up at its distorted image—the sunny schooner from which she came. "I came to see the damage that was done and the treasures that prevail," she tells us.

The shipwreck is the left world where patriarchy ruled and reigned its havoc, and the ocean is the world in which there lurks the possibility of becoming. The poem aspires to cast away the old myths in search of the new: "the thing I came for / the wreck and not the story of the wreck / the thing itself and not the myth . . . in which our names do not appear."

# MARRIAGE

## SONG FOR THE LAST ACT
### Louise Bogan

It is a few months before Thanksgiving and the holidays. A time that reminds me of what I have longed for since before I can remember: a family. I walk along the streets on the Upper West Side and it seems as if every woman my age is pregnant, or maybe I just hadn't been paying attention before. I notice couples my age walking hand in hand, window shopping. I go on Sunday afternoons to an Italian café smelling of roasted beans for a cappuccino, bringing with me a manuscript to edit or a book to read, but I find sitting at the small café table that I can't focus on the page. Instead I listen to the sound of an Italian opera coming through the speakers and look around at couples at other tables seemingly enjoying themselves and I find myself longing for a certain closeness and intimacy I haven't yet found. I am twenty-eight years old and rapidly realizing that I may not find it. The heroines I always worshipped in literature, I've lately come to dislike or not quite feel the same empathy for them I once did. Why didn't Anna Karenina recognize that eventually Vronsky would grow weary of exile from society and tire of her? Madame Bovary is overly sentimental, a fool. Why do Jean Rhys's and Kate Chopin's protagonists die in the face of love? And Daisy Buchanan, shouldn't she get her comeuppance? Katherine Mansfield's bleak stories of loneliness and disconnection leave me in despair. Why should passion be sacrifice? Mr. Darcy doesn't exist. I listen to birds chirp outside my window, drunk on berries, as if they are lusting for something impossible to have.

I become more immersed in my work as an editor, and on the weekends I translate my heartache and despair into lines of poems. It is the only way I know to distract myself from loneliness. At work in the mornings I sort through the stacks of mail (this was in the days before email). One day, a man whom I knew vaguely in high school writes to me care of the publishing house where I work. Years ago, during a summer home from college, a mutual friend of ours and I go to visit him in the country outside of Cleveland where he is living, taking time off from college to work on a novel. We spend hours talking and when it is time to leave I feel a tug of regret. Since then we lost touch. He writes to say he read a poem of mine published in a literary magazine. He lives in Boston and is working at a think tank on a secret project. He invites me to come to stay with him in Cambridge for the weekend. He mentions there is an attic room in his house where I can write my poems. I'm intrigued. I slide into hope, and after we exchange more letters, I eventually decide to go. We spend a long weekend together sharing memories from high school, connecting over stories about our parents, our siblings, and our high school relationships that had outworn their welcome and gone on too long. We take walks with his dog across the bridge over the Charles and watch the rowers. Wander into used bookstores. Drink dark cups of espresso and later wine. A crack in the universe is opening, but I sense something I want to ignore. Why is this man living in this huge house, big enough for a family, on his own? Something isn't right. I push aside my doubts. After the weekend is over I reluctantly return to my small studio apartment in New York City and relive the experience in my mind as it slowly evolves into wistfulness, holding on to words that were said and promises made and ponder if what I felt between us was real. I wonder if he sensed how lonely and desperate I've become. Does it show in my face, trap itself in the spaces between my words, hide in the tender compartments of my body?

Our ten-year high school reunion is approaching over Thanksgiving weekend. The plan is to meet again there in Cleveland. Still, I wonder as each day passes why he hasn't called. In the hotel lobby where the reunion is held, I position myself near the entrance and peer over shoulders and heads. I remind myself that I'm a poet and editor living in New York. I'm dressed in stylish black stretch pants, flowing black silk blouse and high boots, but inside I'm still the uncomfortable-in-my-skin, awkward girl from Cleveland willing the man from Cambridge to walk through the door. He never shows. Maybe I had imagined the encounter? Maybe he was a ghost of my austere imagination? As the night wears on, my spirits sink. Then, in walks another man. I vaguely remember him from high school. He's wearing a navy-blue turtleneck, a jacket, and black jeans and has a friendly, slightly ironic smile and clay-colored eyes that exude warmth and generosity. He's down-to-earth, present, not a ghost. A former athlete, he's in his second year of law school. I don't know what it is about him exactly. He seems more grown-up than the men I've been dating. He's sound and practical, with a vision for his future. He offers to drive me home in the wintery, snowy twilight, his car occasionally sliding on the road, and when I say goodbye to him, on a lark I reach over and kiss him on the cheek, and it is sealed. Two years later we marry.

The first year of our marriage he's a young associate at a firm. I am an associate editor publishing my poems in literary magazines and shopping around a first book of poetry. On weekends and evenings he studies for the bar exam. I read manuscripts and work on my poems and write what seems like hundreds of drafts of a first novel. We live in a studio apartment the size of a closet. At night we drink cheap wine and eat bowls of pasta. A year later, celebrating our hard-earned raises, we graduate to a fourth floor one-bedroom walk-up with views into a back garden. In the garden are vines of wisteria and a cherry tree, and pink and blue hydrangeas that bloom at the beginning of summer. Though we have only five hundred square feet to call our own in this vast city, it feels like paradise. It is only the beginning.

We celebrate anniversaries, births, bar mitzvahs, and graduations; a first book publication, the formation of a law firm, signing of a mortgage for a new apartment, deaths of loved ones. Together we endure days of joy and disappointment, loss, ill parents, setbacks, small victories, and distresses. Ten, twenty years pass. We attend the wedding of a cousin's son and his bride in their early thirties and for a moment I

can't catch my breath. Were we ever that young and inno-
cent? We witness this lovely couple say their scared vows in a
Catholic church and throughout the autumnal afternoon, rel-
ish in its warm afterglow. They look so hopeful and full of
promise, two lovers swooning into the embrace of the future,
dedicating themselves to something beyond the external noise
of politics, protests, and injustices that fill the newspapers and
incite the media. I think about all that is waiting before them,
how each milestone will change them in ways that in this mo-
ment, as they look into each other's eyes, are impossible to
comprehend. How do we commemorate the daily rituals of
getting up each morning to the familiar sound of the alarm
clock, the creak of the shower turning on, the briefcase click-
ing shut, the meals across the table, disappointments, and
quarrels as we evolve as a couple across the passage of time?
How does the quotidian shape our psychic lives? What mys-
teries lie in togetherness?

## SONG FOR THE LAST ACT
### Louise Bogan (1897–1970)

Now that I have your face by heart, I look
Less at its features than its darkening frame
Where quince and melon, yellow as young flame,
Lie with quilled dahlias and the shepherd's crook.
Beyond, a garden. There, in insolent ease
The lead and marble figures watch the show
Of yet another summer loath to go
Although the scythes hang in the apple trees.

Now that I have your face by heart, I look.

Now that I have your voice by heart, I read

In the black chords upon a dulling page
Music that is not meant for music's cage,
Whose emblems mix with words that shake and
    bleed.
The staves are shuttled over with a stark
Unprinted silence. In a double dream
I must spell out the storm, the running stream.
The beat's too swift. The notes shift in the dark.

Now that I have your voice by heart, I read.

Now that I have your heart by heart, I see
The wharves with their great ships and architraves;
The rigging and the cargo and the slaves
On a strange beach under a broken sky.
O not departure, but a voyage done!
The bales stand on the stone; the anchor weeps
Its red rust downward, and the long vine creeps
Beside the salt herb, in the lengthening sun.

Now that I have your heart by heart, I see.

———

"Song for the Last Act" memorializes the breadth of uncon-
ditional, sometimes irrational love. It exemplifies how we

mysteriously "shift in the dark" as it documents the passage of two lives spent together and the ways in which this union allows us "to read," "to look," "to see" in a different key.

Poet Richard Howard called Louise Bogan "the best American woman poet between Dickinson and Bishop." I discover her bewitching poems in an all-women poetry seminar at the University of Iowa chaired by the poet Carol Muske-Dukes. In that classroom we probe the ways in which Bogan's poems articulate unsaid truths and conundrums about the interior lives of women.

The poet Marianne Moore said of her poems: "Louise Bogan's art is compactness compacted. Emotion with her, as she has said of certain fiction, is 'itself form, the kernel which builds outward form from inward intensity.'"

# GRIEF

## MUSÉE DES BEAUX ARTS
W. H. Auden
## ONE ART
Elizabeth Bishop

My youngest sister takes her life at twenty-one. She is my mother's last child, who once renewed our spirits and for a time saved my mother's second marriage. I am blindsided and heartbroken. I am thirty-one, married, an editor and poet living in New York City, pregnant with my first child, my own life slowly coming together. All in an instant, a dark wind, the hand of a brutal heaven, has knocked me out. From one moment to another the world has changed and I am no longer safe. No one I love is. How did this happen? Where did everything go wrong? Why hadn't we known? The questions swirl around me creating a vortex I can't climb out of. How is this possible? I think of my childhood friend Marie, who also took her own life, beautiful girls nearly the same age at the precipice of becoming. There are no words. I cannot speak about it for years.

What happened? people ask. I have no answers. I have entered the world of *I don't know*. It is unrecoverable. No one close to her understood she was suicidal, and the night she carries out her death wish, perhaps hoping to be found, that flicker of hope to sustain her is not available. The loss of this bright, beautiful girl who transformed my childhood is unreal and at times unendurable. She is in my dreams. My memories. I see her everywhere. In the faces of young women on the subway or those I pass on the street. I am in a state of disbelief and shock; it seems as if I'm not quite living, but existing in another country marked by grief. We sit shiva for a week, gathering in my childhood home to receive visitors. When it is time to return to work, it is as if I am navigating a strange new land. I'm worried about my mother and how she'll go on. She never fully recovers. How could she? Among friends or colleagues, I go through the motions, but I'm not quite there. I'm an onlooker, lost in a dark wood and I wonder if I will ever again be able to find my way out and return to the daily, unburdened life I once led. It is as if there is an invisible wall separating me from others.

## MUSÉE DES BEAUX ARTS
### W. H. Auden (1907–1973)

About suffering they were never wrong,
The Old Masters: how well they understood
Its human position; how it takes place

While someone else is eating or opening a window or just
    walking dully along;
How, when the aged are reverently, passionately waiting
For the miraculous birth, there always must be
Children who did not specially want it to happen, skating
On a pond at the edge of the wood:
They never forgot
That even the dreadful martyrdom must run its course
Anyhow in a corner, some untidy spot
Where the dogs go on with their doggy life and the
    torturer's horse
Scratches its innocent behind on a tree.

In Breughel's Icarus, for instance: how everything
    turns away
Quite leisurely from the disaster; the ploughman may
Have heard the splash, the forsaken cry,
But for him it was not an important failure; the sun shone
As it had to on the white legs disappearing into the green
Water; and the expensive delicate ship that must have seen
Something amazing, a boy failing out of the sky,
Had somewhere to get to and sailed calmly on.

———

W. H. Auden documents the otherworldly state of grief and
tragedy; how it strikes families while others are doing the
dishes or taking the dog for a walk. Even dogs continue on
their doggy life. The poem is inspired by a trip to the Musée

des Beaux Arts, where Auden came across the painting *Land-scape with the Fall of Icarus* by Peter Brueghel the Elder. The poem contains two storylines. First is the story of the speaker recounting the wisdom and knowledge of the Old Masters, the painters who understood the nature of suffering and loss—that it happens internally. Second is the story of the myth of Icarus, the subject of Brueghel's painting. In the myth Daedalus and his son, Icarus, are imprisoned in the labyrinth by King Menlos. Daedalus makes two pairs of wings out of feathers and wax. He gives one pair to his son and cautions him that flying too close to the sun will cause the wax to melt. Icarus becomes ecstatic with his ability to fly and forgets his father's warning. He flies too near the sun and plunges to his death in the sea.

In the painting, Brueghel depicts the onlookers, the ploughman who hears the splash of Icarus hitting the sea, and all those for whom the loss is not personally important, and shows how they turn away. Perhaps in the poem Auden meant for us to see how unimportant we are as individuals in relation to the universe. Or perhaps he meant it ironically—that each loss and the onslaught of grief are particular only to the mourner. For instance, how can anyone else know what it's like to see my sister's wildflower blue eyes look up at me?

In an interview in the *Paris Review*, Auden was asked if he had any aids for inspiration. He did not have high-minded ideas of the muse or of poetry in general. He hoped that the reader might find his or her journey in his poetry. "Poetry is not self-expression," he said. "Each of us, of course, has a unique perspective, which we hope to communicate. We hope that someone reading it will say, 'Of course, I knew that all the time but never realized it before.' "

I read. I go to movies. I see art. I work. I write. I call my mother long distance. Have dinners with my sisters. I slide into my husband's arms at night and I let "dreadful martyrdom" run its course. I don't know where the pain and grief go. Sometimes it materializes in subconscious anger and resentment. Other times it is as if it burrows into the corners and at moments when I am least aware jumps out. I stuff it back. I will spend years trying to capture the experience of suicide in a prose work, a book that I eventually publish. Poems remain a sustaining source of comfort. This poem that I have known for ages suddenly takes on new power and meaning. I find myself sometimes at night in bed, unable to sleep, reciting its lines in my head as if to master it.

## ONE ART

Elizabeth Bishop (1911–1979)

The art of losing isn't hard to master;
so many things seem filled with the intent
to be lost that their loss is no disaster.

Lose something every day. Accept the fluster
of lost door keys, the hour badly spent.
The art of losing isn't hard to master.

Then practice losing farther, losing faster:
places, and names, and where it was you meant
to travel. None of these will bring disaster.

I lost my mother's watch. And look! my last, or
next-to-last, of three loved houses went.
The art of losing isn't hard to master.

I lost two cities, lovely ones. And, vaster,
some realms I owned, two rivers, a continent.
I miss them, but it wasn't a disaster.

—Even losing you (the joking voice, a gesture
I love) I shan't have lied. It's evident
the art of losing's not too hard to master
though it may look like (*Write* it!) like disaster.

———

Elizabeth Bishop's poetry abounds with concrete and vivid details of the ordinary world and is infused with a powerful sense of morality. Her father died before she was a year old. When Elizabeth Bishop was five, her mother, suffering from mental instability, was committed to an institution. It is not surprising, given her losses, that many of her poems are about grief, longing, loneliness, and exile. She is known for a clear, cool voice wrought with emotion.

"One Art" is a poem that documents the journey of loss through dark irony and humor. It is written in the form of a villanelle, a nineteen-line verse poem with a rigid rhyme

scheme that repeats certain end words and refrains, assigning
it complex musicality. Its power is restraint. The rhyme se-
quence allows for its song-like quality and its surface charm.
It racks up its losses from the more superficial, such as keys
and watches, to houses, and to rivers and to cities, to the more
profound loss of losing a loved one. The ironic last lines,
"even losing you isn't hard to master," suggests our ability to
overcome even the most monumental of losses, for each pass-
ing day, the poem reminds us is a loss in itself. Of Bishop's
poetry, the novelist Colm Tóibín has said, "For her, the most
difficult thing to do was to make a statement; around these
statements in her poems she created a hard-won aura, strange
sad acceptance that this statement was all that could be said.
Or maybe there was something more, but it had escaped her.
This space between what there was and what could be made
certain or held fast often made her tone playful, in the way as
a feather applied gently to the inner nostril makes you sneeze
in a way that is amused as much as pained."

# SUICIDE

## TULIPS
Sylvia Plath

## WAKING IN THE BLUE
Robert Lowell

Losing a loved one is devastating, but suicide, the act of taking one's own life, is irreconcilable. I don't understand it or know what to do with it. I'm angry. Not at my sister, but at all I don't understand of the human psyche and the forces that unwillingly impinge upon a life. I don't know what to do with this knot of fury. As I go about my day, it often feels like I'm stepping over land mines and not knowing when one will erupt. I read to try to understand. It's more than depression that causes someone to take her life. Otherwise, everyone suffering from severe depression would end her life. It is a state of mind that gets locked in, I think. Only the poets seem to provide insight into the mystery of this form of suffering. Sylvia Plath's poems take on more meaning and depth. I mine them for similarities and answers. It seems to me that for some people the desire to come apart will be as strong, if not stronger, than the desire to stay whole. Every day, I ask myself how I will get through this brutal loss. Poetry, work, love, friendship, the sight of the waves crashing in the ocean, the piney scent of the October air offer occasional refuge. Eventually I find comfort in the idea that there are no clear answers. Poetry offers consolation and knowledge but it cannot reverse fate and bring my sister back.

## TULIPS

### Sylvia Plath

The tulips are too excitable, it is winter here.
Look how white everything is, how quiet, how snowed-in.
I am learning peacefulness, lying by myself quietly
As the light lies on these white walls, this bed, these hands.
I am nobody; I have nothing to do with explosions.
I have given my name and my day-clothes up to the nurses
And my history to the anesthetist and my body to surgeons.

They have propped my head between the pillow and the
     sheet-cuff
Like an eye between two white lids that will not shut.
Stupid pupil, it has to take everything in.
The nurses pass and pass, they are no trouble,
They pass the way gulls pass inland in their white caps,
Doing things with their hands, one just the same as another,
So it is impossible to tell how many there are.

My body is a pebble to them, they tend it as water
Tends to the pebbles it must run over, smoothing them gently.

They bring me numbness in their bright needles, they bring
     me sleep.
Now I have lost myself I am sick of baggage— —
My patent leather overnight case like a black pillbox,
My husband and child smiling out of the family photo;
Their smiles catch onto my skin, little smiling hooks.

I have let things slip, a thirty-year-old cargo boat
Stubbornly hanging on to my name and address.
They have swabbed me clear of my loving associations.
Scared and bare on the green plastic-pillowed trolley
I watched my teaset, my bureaus of linen, my books
Sink out of sight, and the water went over my head.
I am a nun now, I have never been so pure.

I didn't want any flowers, I only wanted
To lie with my hands turned up and be utterly empty.
How free it is, you have no idea how free— —
The peacefulness is so big it dazes you,
And it asks nothing, a name tag, a few trinkets.
It is what the dead close on, finally; I imagine them
Shutting their mouths on it, like a Communion tablet.

The tulips are too red in the first place, they hurt me.
Even through the gift paper I could hear them breathe
Lightly, through their white swaddlings, like an awful baby.
Their redness talks to my wound, it corresponds.
They are subtle: they seem to float, though they weigh me down,
Upsetting me with their sudden tongues and their color,
A dozen red lead sinkers round my neck.

Nobody watched me before, now I am watched.
The tulips turn to me, and the window behind me
Where once a day the light slowly widens and slowly thins,
And I see myself, flat, ridiculous, a cut-paper shadow
Between the eye of the sun and the eyes of the tulips,
And I have no face, I have wanted to efface myself.
The vivid tulips eat my oxygen.

Before they came the air was calm enough,
Coming and going, breath by breath, without any fuss.
Then the tulips filled it up like a loud noise.
Now the air snags and eddies round them the way a river
Snags and eddies round a sunken rust-red engine.
They concentrate my attention, that was happy
Playing and resting without committing itself.

The walls, also, seem to be warming themselves.
The tulips should be behind bars like dangerous animals;
They are opening like the mouth of some great African cat,
And I am aware of my heart: it opens and closes
Its bowl of red blooms out of sheer love of me.
The water I taste is warm and salt, like the sea,
And comes from a country far away as health.

———

"Tulips" depicts this state where one is powerless to the terrible tide of darkness. Depression is a disease that doctors and nurses must attend to gently, "like water" rushing over a pebble. The poem is about a stay in the hospital after a suicide attempt and bears witness to the interior mind of an individual so overcome with melancholy it is as if she exists in a different country from healthy people. The speaker in the poem looks at the photograph of her husband and child by her bedside and their "smiles catch onto her skin, little smiling hooks." She is aware, in her depressive state, of the intense divide between them, and the shame she bears for her failing. Her face is "flat, ridiculous," she wants to "efface" herself. With its dark and gorgeous lyricism, the poem moves lethargically, quietly down the page, echoing the state of mind of its speaker.

Plath's poetry is characterized by potent imagery, a brilliant imagination, and a heightened and intense awareness of the evolving self. Plath wrote about painful subjects: suicide, self-hatred, unstable relationships, Nazis. Her controlled use of image and keen sense of dramatic tension and structure draw the reader into the place of suffering. Conflating poet and speaker, expression and gravity, genuine confessions and dark irony, Plath's poems document versions of the unreachable and unknowable self. "Tulips" navigates this shadowy, alienating netherworld of mental pain and the fine line between survival and death.

## WAKING IN THE BLUE
### Robert Lowell (1917–1977)

The night attendant, a B.U. sophomore,
rouses from the mare's-nest of his drowsy head
propped on *The Meaning of Meaning*.

He catwalks down our corridor.
Azure day
makes my agonized blue window bleaker.
Crows maunder on the petrified fairway.
Absence! My heart grows tense
as though a harpoon were sparring for the kill.
(This is the house for the "mentally ill.")

What use is my sense of humor?
I grin at Stanley, now sunk in his sixties,
once a Harvard all-American fullback,
(if such were possible!)
still hoarding the build of a boy in his twenties,
as he soaks, a ramrod
with the muscle of a seal
in his long tub,
vaguely urinous from the Victorian plumbing.
A kingly granite profile in a crimson gold-cap,
worn all day, all night,
he thinks only of his figure,
of slimming on sherbert and ginger ale—
more cut off from words than a seal.
This is the way day breaks in Bowditch
       Hall at McLean's;
the hooded night lights bring out "Bobbie,"
Porcelain '29,
a replica of Louis XVI
without the wig—
redolent and roly-poly as a sperm whale,

as he swashbuckles about in his birthday suit
and horses at chairs.

These victorious figures of bravado ossified young.

In between the limits of day,
hours and hours go by under the crew haircuts
and slightly too little nonsensical bachelor twinkle
of the Roman Catholic attendants.
(There are no Mayflower
screwballs in the Catholic Church.)

After a hearty New England breakfast,
I weigh two hundred pounds
this morning. Cock of the walk,
I strut in my turtle-necked French sailor's jersey
before the metal shaving mirrors,
and see the shaky future grow familiar
in the pinched, indigenous faces
of these thoroughbred mental cases,
twice my age and half my weight.
We are all old-timers,
each of us holds a locked razor.

———

"Waking in the Blue" opens with a night attendant, a sopho-
more in college, on the ward of a psychiatric hospital, asleep,
propped on a textbook called *The Meaning of Meaning*, a text
used in many fields of language, philosophy, linguistics, and

cognitive science. The text, a mere prop in the poem, is inadequate in the ward. It belies the paradoxical world of mental agony, where abstract meaning, contextualized in many sciences, vanishes into the ether of illness.

Though Lowell suffered from manic depression, after many hospitalizations during his adult life, he died of natural causes. "Waking in the Blue," from his influential work *Life Studies*, is an example of the emerging confessional poetry of his era. In excruciating and horrific detail it depicts the speaker's candid awareness of how his mental illness afflicts him and how even those we may least suspect—the "Harvard all-American fullback," for instance—are susceptible to its cruel powers. Everyone on the ward holds "a locked razor."

Michael Schmidt, in *Lives of the Poets*, calls his work "a poetry of symptoms"—"illness, false health, false hope, failure—and love." Many of his poems, including "Waking in the Blue," derive from his suffering and illness. Lowell began taking lithium at the age of fifty. Saskia Hamilton, the editor of Lowell's *Letters*, said, "Lithium treatment relieved him from suffering the idea that he was morally and emotionally responsible for the fact that he relapsed. However, it did not entirely prevent relapses. And he was troubled and anxious about the impact of his relapses on his family and friends until the end of his life."

The poet John Berryman, a contemporary and friend of Robert Lowell's, also suffered from intense bouts of depression. When he was twelve his father took his own life, an event that haunted his poetry. In his poem "Freshman Blues," he articulates how the legacy of our parents shapes us, even after death:

Thought I much then on perforated daddy,
daddy boxed in & let down with strong straps,
when I my friends' homes, visited, with fathers
universal & intact . . .

Shocking, darkly funny, tragic, my eye travels to the phrase "universal & intact" as the prevailing experience a child covets. In this era of confessional poetry, Sylvia Plath, John Berryman, Robert Lowell, and Anne Sexton all suffered from corrosive mental pain. Of the four poets, Lowell was the only one who did not take his own life.

In a letter to John Berryman, Lowell writes: "I have been thinking about you all summer and how we have gone through the same troubles, visiting the bottom of the world . . . the dark moment comes, it goes."

# MOTHERHOOD

THE POMEGRANATE
  Eavan Boland
ON MY FIRST SON
  Ben Jonson
FUNERAL BLUES
  W. H. Auden
NICK AND THE CANDLESTICK
  Sylvia Plath

My first child is a daughter. I remember exactly the day we conceived. It was in the early hours of New Year's Day after returning home from a long, snow-filled walk from lower Manhattan (impossible to get a cab on New Year's Eve) where we celebrated the New Year eating bowls of pasta and sharing a bottle of Chianti at a local Italian restaurant. I know I am pregnant almost instantly. I've wanted to be a mother for as long as I can remember, hoping to create for my child the stable childhood that was stolen from me when my own father died. For months before she is born, I imagine her. We have our own secret language. When we are alone, lying on the couch or taking a walk in the park I feel her move to the rhythm of my breath. She hiccups when I do. I feel her blood churning in mine, changing the chemistry of my breathing, my digestion, the way I talk and feel. My stomach looks like I'm hiding a bowling ball underneath my sweater. It's hard and full and when I walk I sometimes cup my hand underneath my panty-line to make sure she doesn't drop. I walk through the park and watch the young children playing in the playground or skating at the ice rink. Do all mothers imagine their daughters to be mini-versions of themselves? I hope she won't have the traits I dislike about myself. I want her to be bright and confident. I am already giving her advice in my own head. I play music for her. I have a library of books all picked out. I walk past baby stores and stare at the mannequins, the little girls dressed in polka dot dresses and Mary Janes. When I give birth prematurely at thirty-two weeks, I know before I see her exactly what she will look like, and I'm right. She has my round face and wide forehead. There are complications and I'm rushed to the operating room for an emergency C-section. Her lungs collapse ten minutes after she is born. Against all we are prepared for, our baby does not survive. The idyllic image I have held of her and our lives together, our family, is shattered. For weeks I can't take it in. It is surely a combination of pregnancy hormones still ruling my body, producing milk in my breasts, making my uterus contract, and my desire to not quite let her go. I refuse to talk to anyone, rapt as I am in my private universe with my daughter, unable to fully accept that she is gone.

# THE POMEGRANATE
## Eavan Boland (1944–)

The only legend I have ever loved is
the story of a daughter lost in hell.
And found and rescued there.
Love and blackmail are the gist of it.
Ceres and Persephone the names.
And the best thing about the legend is
I can enter it anywhere. And have.
As a child in exile in
a city of fogs and strange consonants,
I read it first and at first I was
an exiled child in the crackling dusk of
the underworld, the stars blighted. Later
I walked out in a summer twilight
searching for my daughter at bed-time.
When she came running I was ready
to make any bargain to keep her.
I carried her back past whitebeams
and wasps and honey-scented buddleias.
But I was Ceres then and I knew
winter was in store for every leaf
on every tree on that road.
Was inescapable for each one we passed.
And for me.
    It is winter
and the stars are hidden.
I climb the stairs and stand where I can see

my child asleep beside her teen magazines,
her can of Coke, her plate of uncut fruit.
The pomegranate! How did I forget it?
She could have come home and been safe
and ended the story and all
our heart-broken searching but she reached
out a hand and plucked a pomegranate.
She put out her hand and pulled down
the French sound for apple and
the noise of stone and the proof
that even in the place of death,
at the heart of legend, in the midst
of rocks full of unshed tears
ready to be diamonds by the time
the story was told, a child can be
hungry. I could warn her. There is still a chance.
The rain is cold. The road is flint-coloured.
The suburb has cars and cable television.
The veiled stars are above ground.
It is another world. But what else
can a mother give her daughter but such
beautiful rifts in time?
If I defer the grief I will diminish the gift.
The legend will be hers as well as mine.
She will enter it. As I have.
She will wake up. She will hold
the papery flushed skin in her hand.
And to her lips. I will say nothing.

———

This poem, by the Irish poet Eavan Boland, articulates the umbilical bond between a mother and a daughter. It is an open-ended poem. Any mother can enter it, whether her child is alive or dead. It takes as its understory the myth of Persephone and Demeter, the mother who lost her daughter to the underworld and bargains her back for half the year. Even after a child dies, a mother continues to live her life through imagination. As each year passes, she thinks of her, of what age she'd be, imagining her among the girls she sees dressed in their school uniforms walking to school, or a girl walking hand in hand with a boy, wondering what she would look like, who she would become. "If I defer the grief, I diminish the gift," Boland expresses, juxtaposing the mythic underworld with the world of the everyday—of Diet Coke and teen magazines and cable television. About this poem and motherhood, Boland writes: "Motherhood was central for me—I mean as a poet, as well as in every other way. 'The Pomegranate' came out of a series of realizations like that. And having said that, I don't think I realized at the beginning how much the perspective of motherhood could affect the poem in strictly aesthetic ways. Take for example the nature poem: when I was young and studying poetry at University I had a very orthodox, nineteenth century view of the nature poem. That the sensibility of the poet was instructed in some moral way by the natural world. And it was an idea I just couldn't use. I couldn't get close to it. But when my daughters were born, that all changed. I no longer felt I was observing nature in some Romantic-poet way. I felt I was right at the center of it: a participant in the whole world of change and renewal. "The Pomegranate" is a sort of nature poem in that way—there's a deeply seasonal aspect to the raising of children. And I wanted to write that."

After a year passes, we decide to try to have another baby. When I become pregnant again it's different. I'm apprehensive. I can't quite take it all in. We take precautions. I'm on bed rest and am given a procedure to prevent premature labor. I am carrying a boy. Alone during the day, friends bring me muffins and coffee and stay for a bit to chat, but I can't really pay attention. I'm already trapped in the otherworld, communing with my little boy. Judy, who comes to clean my house, helps me now with groceries and meals. As she is dusting the bedroom, she tells me that more than one clock in a room means death. There is an alarm clock propped on the nightstand like a little soldier of attention and on my bookshelf, a small Tiffany silver clock, a wedding gift commemorating the passing of time with elegant Roman numerals. I am propped on one side to keep the nutrients flowing for the baby and ask Judy to take the Tiffany clock and put it in the living room. Once she leaves and the apartment is quiet again, an ominous shadow descends, and the room darkens, though it's not quite four. I am obsessed with my pregnancy. I look in the mirror when I get up to go the bathroom and worry that I am carrying small. When I was pregnant with my daughter, I was almost twice the size. The next morning, Judy tells me that boys carry differently than girls, but I don't believe her. I call the doctor because now I think I don't remember the last time I felt the baby move. I press my hand on the lower part of my abdomen to see if he will respond, but there is no movement. It all happens quickly. I'm in a cab, then the doctor's office getting a stress test, and within the hour in the cool antiseptic operating room of the hospital being prepped for a C-section. It turns out that all the hours of lying on one side was futile. The baby isn't getting enough nutrients and has to come out of the compressed womb of my birthwater into the light of day to grow in an incubator. It is too soon. My boy is born at twenty-six weeks. He's so tiny you could hold him in one hand, and yet his features are unmistakably those of my husband's. Within twenty-four hours, his kidneys fail him. "My sin was too much hope of thee," writes Ben Jonson, a contemporary of Shakespeare, in this moving exploration of the loss of a son.

## ON MY FIRST SON
### Ben Jonson (1572–1637)

Farewell, thou child of my right hand, and joy;
My sin was too much hope of thee, loved boy.
Seven years thou'wert lent to me, and I thee pay,
Exacted by thy fate, on the just day.
O could I lose all father now! for why
Will man lament the state he should envy?
To have so soon 'scaped world's and flesh's rage,
And, if no other misery, yet age?

Rest in soft peace, and asked, say, "Here doth lie
Ben Jonson his best piece of poetry."
For whose sake henceforth all his vows be such
As what he loves may never like too much.

One day or seven years. No matter. We've already imagined days in the park, a toddler tossing a ball, a boy on the living room rug playing with his trucks. "On My First Son" seeks meaning when no meaning is available. Perhaps we turn to poetry because it can fathom and hold the inexplicable, the gasp between words, the emotional hues impossible to capture in everyday speech or conversation. I can't stop thinking about what Judy said. I take the Tiffany clock and put it in a drawer. I cannot look at it. Lines from Auden's funeral poem, "Funeral Blues," with its first line, "Stop all the clocks, cut off the telephone," take on more meaning.

## FUNERAL BLUES
### W. H. Auden

Stop all the clocks, cut off the telephone,
Prevent the dog from barking with a juicy bone,
Silence the pianos and with muffled drum
Bring out the coffin, let the mourners come.

Let aeroplanes circle moaning overhead
Scribbling on the sky the message He Is Dead,

Put crêpe bows round the white necks of the public doves,
Let the traffic policemen wear black cotton gloves.

He was my North, my South, my East and West,
My working week and my Sunday rest,
My noon, my midnight, my talk, my song;
I thought that love would last for ever: I was wrong.

The stars are not wanted now: put out every one;
Pack up the moon and dismantle the sun;
Pour away the ocean and sweep up the wood;
For nothing now can ever come to any good.

When the babies died I lost the ability to raise them, but I am still a mother. I have given birth to two children. For years, I burn with envy every time I see a newborn child. It is impossible to be around friends with young children without inhabiting the spaces where my own losses and desires lay. I wish I could be a better person and rise above it, but that kind of stoic grace is not available to me. It's like being hungry all the time and never invited to the feast. When my third child is born full-term, healthy, from the gifted womb and dividing cells of another woman's body, I can't take my eyes off of him. When we bring him home, we have nothing. Not a crib, not a diaper, not a onesie or a bottle or a stroller. We are still living in the aftermath of ravaged promise. When we saw our son for the first time, my husband was convinced something was wrong with him, he didn't seem to have a chin, until the doctor told us that no newborns have chins, that is how far away from hope we had traveled.

When we finally bring our baby home, sorrow for the two children we will never see again and joy for the one secure in my arms are intertwined; they cannot be separated. There's something else. My psyche will not quite allow itself to feel the happiness and love that is flooding through every cell in my body. I keep expecting something terrible to happen. Days pass. I feed and diaper, bathe and swaddle, but mostly spend hours watching him, his eyes closed like two little commas or upside down slivers of moon. I like his solid weight in my arms. It's like nothing I've ever felt before. I like the way his little fingers curl around mine. His hot-to-the-touch skin. I am selfish and voracious. I want to be the only one to hold him. It takes months before the fear of losing him goes away. Like the speaker in this magical poem by Sylvia Plath, I am a miner, excavating a rich new world, but always now with hesitation and awareness of life's fragility.

## NICK AND THE CANDLESTICK
### Sylvia Plath

I am a miner. The light burns blue.
Waxy stalactites
Drip and thicken, tears

The earthen womb
Exudes from its dead boredom.
Black bat airs

Wrap me, raggy shawls,
Cold homicides.
They weld to me like plums.

Old cave of calcium
Icicles, old echoer.
Even the newts are white,

Those holy Joes.
And the fish, the fish—
Christ! they are panes of ice,

A vice of knives,
A piranha
Religion, drinking

Its first communion out of my live toes.
The candle
Gulps and recovers its small altitude,

Its yellows hearten.
O love, how did you get here?
O embryo

Remembering, even in sleep,
Your crossed position.
The blood blooms clean

In you, ruby.
The pain
You wake to is not yours.

Love, love,
I have hung our cave with roses,
With soft rugs——

The last of Victoriana.
Let the stars
Plummet to their dark address,

Let the mercuric
Atoms that cripple drip
Into the terrible well,

You are the one
Solid the spaces lean on, envious.
You are the baby in the barn.

———

"Nick and the Candlestick," its title mimicking a nursery rhyme, is personal, though it also carries biblical and universal overtones. Images of beauty, love, and resiliency reverberate in the lines. "You are the one / Solid the spaces lean on, envious. / You are the baby in the barn," Plath writes, seeing within her own child infinity and grace. For her, and perhaps all mothers, this baby is a miracle, biblical, "the baby in the barn." The poet is the "miner" exploring this new world of motherhood, awaking in the first light of a blue dawn to find her son in a "crossed position" in his crib. "Oh love, how did you get here," she remarks. How is this miracle possible? "The pain you wake to is not yours," the poem reverberates, prophetically aware of the history mothers pass on to their children.

The poem becomes more poignant when we consider Plath's history. Fifty some years ago she took her life in her flat in London at the age of thirty-one. Her children, Frieda, three, and Nicholas, barely one, slept in the next room. She stuffed towels underneath the space in the door, left milk on the table in the other room for them, knowing the nanny was on her way, and turned on the gas oven and lay her head inside. At the time she was separated from her husband, the English poet Ted Hughes, who was living with another woman. Plath, a young wife, was instrumental in placing her husband's first book, *The Hawk in the Rain*, with a publisher in 1957, the year I was born. She typed out almost all of his poems and submitted them to a competition judged by W. H. Auden, Stephen Spender, and Marianne Moore, where it was awarded the prize and published by Harper and Row. Their work and their professional identity were intricately linked. The night Plath ended her life she had been lonely and perhaps still in love with her husband. It was a cold winter to be alone with two young children. Her mind that night got the better of her. In the months before Plath died, in the early hours of the dawn, she wrote several dozen of the most unforgettable and profound poems in the English language. "Nick and the Candlestick" is one of those poems.

Perhaps anticipating her critics, she said of her poetics: "I believe that one should be able to control and manipulate experiences, even the most terrifying—like madness, being tortured, this kind of experience—and one should be able to manipulate these experiences with an informed and intelligent mind. I think that personal experience shouldn't be a kind of shut box and mirror-looking narcissistic experience. I believe it should be generally relevant, to such things as Hiroshima and Dachau, and so on."

Plath carried out her own dictum. The intensity of feeling she achieved in her work comes from her poetic control, intelligence, and bravery. Her mastery of metaphor—like the metaphor of the cave in "Nick and the Candlestick" that represents that deep and enclosed and hitherto unknown intimacy between mother and child—extends the poem into another realm. Plath seeks to universalize her experience, to in effect, "render impersonal the (apparently) intense personal." Some critics have denounced her poetics because of its elements of pathology and brutality. I find it impossible to question her poetic mastery.

# TERROR

## TRY TO PRAISE THE MUTILATED WORLD
### Adam Zagejewski

One morning in early September I take the bus with my son to drop him off at school on 111th and Amsterdam. He is five years old with blond hair so fine it attracts static, and a personality that is alive, present, and engaged. We can barely walk down the street without him tugging my hand to stop at a shop window or hop up on a bench. When we ride the bus he's looking out the window, watching the passersby. I drop him off at the bottom of the porch steps of his school and my heart catches when he stops before entering the building to wave goodbye. By eight thirty or nine, I'm at my desk at the publishing house office in midtown, drinking my first cup of coffee, starting up my computer when my phone rings. It's my sister who works at a gallery uptown. "Are you OK?" She asks after my husband and then the phone goes dead. Outside my office door colleagues are congregating in the hallway. Something's happening. I look out the window. Smoke envelops the blue sky. A colleague says something about a building collapsing downtown. A plane. Through the window, sirens blare and fire engines scream down Fifth Avenue. My husband's office is across the street from the World Trade Center. The phone call from my sister clicks in. I begin to panic. I reach for the phone to call him. No signal. I go into the office across the hall to find out more about what has happened. A colleague is watching a report of the incident on his computer. Falling debris and flying paper swirl in the air. We see one tower collapsing, folding in on itself like an accordion. Flames and smoke form their own ghostly tower where the building once stood.

Outside people are running and shoving. The city is in a state of panic. Colleagues pack up and vacate the office. I don't know where my husband is but I know that if he's OK I'll find him at my son's school, the Cathedral School of St. John the Divine, uptown. I walk down the flights of stairs, afraid to use the elevator, and follow the stampede heading up Fifth Avenue to escape the pandemonium of lower Manhattan. It is impossible to get a cab or get on a bus and for those moments it's as if the city and its inhabitants are all one and the same. Then miraculously a cab filled with three other passengers stops and lets me in. One of the passengers says that the plane crash was intentional and a terrorist attack. I don't know if this is true or not or what to think. Everything is happening in the moment.

It seems like hours before we make it uptown and the cab drops me off on Amsterdam Avenue. I turn into the close of the cathedral, where hundreds of other parents have gone to fetch their children being let out to parents or caregivers on the porch of the school. Several parents of children of the school work in the towers and there is a strange hush about what's happened so as not to scare the children. I spot my son's blond head of hair shining in the sun, his navy blue pants and white polo shirt with the school emblem over his heart, and break into a sweat of relief. I sweep him into my arms and hold him close. Minutes later, my husband arrives, we all embrace, and I break into tears. White powder from the dust of the tower is on his clothes. His face is ashen and he's trembling. I've never seen him this way before. He witnessed the collapse of the first tower and saw people jumping out of the tower to escape the flames. Once he's found us, he ushers us along, not wanting to linger, anxious to get us safely home. But is any one of us safe anymore?

The sky on the Upper West Side, one hundred blocks away from the horrific assault is monstrously blue. The wind carries the whiff of death. The sounds of sirens blaring and ambulances ripping through the streets lasts throughout the rest of the day and night. Later we will learn that nearly three thousand innocent people were killed in the terrorist attacks of 9/11, many of them men and women who did nothing that morning other than wake up and go to their places of employment. Fear has cast a pall over our city. Life will never be the same. I remember it all, and especially the relief I felt when I saw the blond head of my son, and minutes later my husband hurrying up the close. Thirteen days after the attack, *The New Yorker* printed "Try to Praise the Mutilated World" in its pages.

## TRY TO PRAISE THE MUTILATED WORLD
### Adam Zagajewski (1945–)

Try to praise the mutilated world.
Remember June's long days,

and wild strawberries, drops of rosé wine.
The nettles that methodically overgrow
the abandoned homesteads of exiles.
You must praise the mutilated world.
You watched the stylish yachts and ships;
one of them had a long trip ahead of it,
while salty oblivion awaited others.
You've seen the refugees going nowhere,
you've heard the executioners sing joyfully.
You should praise the mutilated world.
Remember the moments when we were together
in a white room and the curtain fluttered.
Return in thought to the concert where music flared.
You gathered acorns in the park in autumn
and leaves eddied over the earth's scars.
Praise the mutilated world
and the gray feather a thrush lost,
and the gentle light that strays and vanishes
and returns.

———

The poem was written a year and half before the attacks and it is eerily prescient. Though its landscape is inspired by a different country, Poland and its Ukranian villages abandoned in the Post-Yalta years Zagajewski observed on a trip with his father, it remarkably mirrors the aftermath of 9/11 as image by image, a June day, stylish yachts and ships, a white room and its billowing curtains, a concert where music flared, telegraphs reasons to go on living in a newly broken world. In the poem, Zagajewski captures what he refers to as the "contest between beauty and disaster." The poem is both terrifying and consoling. Of the poem, Zagajewski writes: "It's the way I have always seen the world. When I was growing up I saw a lot of ruins in postwar Poland. This is my landscape. Somehow it stayed with me, this feeling that the world is wounded or mutilated and that its executioners sing joyfully."

When the towers tumbled at the World Trade Center this poem about a militated world after terrorism offered Americans a way to move forward among the deluge. Readers posted it on their refrigerators, on bulletin boards, and websites as communities gathered bringing bottles of water and provisions to shelters, hospitals, the Red Cross and to firefighters. All of us who were in New York City will remember the glaringly perfect blue skies of that day, so incongruous with the terrorists' act, and the overall atmosphere of disbelief as the vibrant city mourned the thousands of loved ones lost, and Americans stood frozen in front of their television sets trying to comprehend the improbable act of destruction while somewhere the executioners sang.

# MORTALITY

## THE CHILD IS FATHER TO THE MAN
Gerard Manley Hopkins
## MY HEART LEAPS UP
William Wordsworth

In the basket of my mother's walker she keeps that day's printed-out menu, which they pass out every morning in the care home where she lives. When I ask her about it she says that this way she can remember what day it is, as the date is printed on top of the menu. Every Thursday she likes getting her nails done. Sometimes when I come to visit our nails are coincidentally painted the same color and this pleases her. She likes going to the hairdresser and attending the films they show every week at the little theater at the care home. When she goes to the movies, she sees her friend Bob and they sit in the front row together and sometimes hold hands. In rows behind them sit their aides. Every week they look forward to it like young lovers.

When I come to visit I take my mother out for lunch or we sit in the little garden outside the care home. I ask her to tell me stories about when she was young. On her finger, she wears the diamond wedding ring my father gave her. Years ago, long after her second marriage had ended, she dug it out of her jewelry drawer and put it on and never took it off again. She also legally changed her name back to the surname of her first husband, my father. She turns the ring around on her finger and sometimes I catch her staring at it in a moment of reflection. She tells the same story of how she met my father. I've heard it hundreds of times, but I don't care. After they fell in love, they poked their fingers with a pin and drew blood and then rubbed their fingers together to symbolize their union. We go through her photo album and the photos elicit other memories. I recognize that if I don't find out all my answers or hear her stories now I never will. She's in her mid-eighties. When I look at her face, still beautiful under its folds of soft skin, and into her brown eyes, I see myself reflected back to me, and a sudden awareness of my own mortality creeps in. I also see something that was never there before, a growing acceptance of her own life and its limitations. I don't know how this has happened but it has. And my own resentments and impatience toward her too have over the years miraculously slipped away. Now I am my mother's keeper. With my sisters, we pick my mother's clothes for her. We set up her doctor's appointments and handle her finances and buy her toothpaste and the extra-soft toilet paper she likes. As once my life depended on her, now hers depends upon me. But still, in her presence I am her daughter, her little girl.

## THE CHILD IS FATHER TO THE MAN

Gerard Manley Hopkins (1844–1889)

'The child is father to the man.'
How can he be? The words are wild.
Suck any sense from that who can:
'The child is father to the man.'
No; what the poet did write ran,
'The man is father to the child.'
'The child is father to the man!'
How *can* he be? The words are wild!

———

"The child is father of the man" is a line taken directly from the poem "My Heart Leaps Up" by William Wordsworth.

## MY HEART LEAPS UP

William Wordsworth

My heart leaps up when I behold
    A rainbow in the sky:
So was it when my life began;
So it is now I am a man;
So be it when I shall grow old,
    Or let me die!
The Child is father of the Man;

And I could wish my days to be
Bound each to each by natural piety.

In the Wordsworth poem the speaker looks upon a rainbow and remembers how he felt as a child and reflects that the child within us gives rise to who we are as adults. The Hopkins poem is born out of his quarrel with Wordsworth's conceit. When I fall into the Hopkins poem as an adult taking care of her mother, I find within it the strange reality that happens as parents age and suddenly the child becomes the caretaker of the parent. And yes, agreed, when this happens it is "wild!" Critics have read the Wordsworth poem as an ode to nature and to Wordsworth's deep connection to the natural world through the life cycle. Poems are often born out of quarrels and quandaries. Hopkins quarrels with Wordsworth, with himself, and with the universe in "The Child is Father to the Man." Hopkins was a complicated person. In *Lives of the Poets*, Michael Schmidt writes, "He became a Catholic against the wishes of his family; a Jesuit against the advice of his friends; a disciple of Scotus against the orthodoxy of his order; he had made himself alone."

# MYSTERY

## TEACHERS
and YOUTH
### W. S. Merwin

When I first wake up in the morning, sometimes the fog of dream is thick and I can't remember for a moment who I am or what I'm meant to be doing. On a frosty morning in November an image of my youngest sister dressed in her powder-blue snowsuit pops into my head. I used to bundle her up in it to take her for a spin in her stroller or to play in the snow. It took ages to put on. Other mornings, I remember her stroking the fur of her black-and-white, beloved cat, Gretel. The quick flicker of her smile. Other days, on awakening, my first thought is of my mother. I fear one day she won't remember me. I think of the babies I have lost and count back to how old they would be. Or I remember something my son said or did. Now he's away in college. In moments of recollection, time is irrelevant. I don't know what it is that pulls me out of my thoughts. Is it the sheath of sun coming through the blinds, or the sudden beep on my iPhone? In that window between sleep and full awakening, doubts, worries, memories, the surreal passage of time creep in, for no particular reason as if these swirls of thoughts and memory lead their own private life inside of us.

## TEACHERS

### W. S. Merwin (1927–)

Pain is in this dark room like many speakers
of a costly set though mute
as here the needle and the turning

the night lengthens it is winter
a new year

what I live for I can seldom believe in
who I love I cannot go to
what I hope is always divided

but I say to myself you are not a child now
if the night is long remember your unimportance
sleep

then toward morning I dream of the first words
of books of voyages
sure tellings that did not start by justifying

yet at one time it seems
had taught me

———

"Teachers" opens in the darkness of the night, where pain turns in silence like a mute turntable. It is winter, a new year. The poet ponders his life and its contradictions. What he lives for, he seldom believes in; whom he loves, he cannot go to; he is always divided. When doubt creeps in, he recognizes he is no longer a child, nor the center of the world; his wishes and desires are not always his own to control. As night turns to morning, they vanish and he remembers his early voyages from his first books, his own first encounters, what they taught him, and how they sustained him. By journey's end he has found tranquility and acceptance.

In 1976, W. S. Merwin moved to Maui, Hawaii, to study Zen Buddhism. He bought an abandoned pineapple plantation that he restored to its natural rain forest ecosystem. "Writing poetry always has to do with how you want to live," he said. In his later poems, he returns to the exploration of the natural world and mourns our separation from it; nature is a grounding force that gives him the tools to embrace and accept quietude. He was awarded the Pulitzer Prize twice, first in 1971 for *The Carrier of Ladders* in which the poem "Teachers" appeared and then in 2009 for *The Shadow of Sirius*, a collection of poems about youth and aging and the mysteries of life. Of its subject, Merwin said, "The shadow of Sirius is pure metaphor, pure imagination. . . . We are the shadow of Sirius . . . the other side is what we never know, the dark, the unknown side that guides us, the mystery, that is always with us too. It gives depth and dimension. . . . Poetry comes out of what you don't know."

# YOUTH

### W. S. Merwin

Through all of youth I was looking for you
without knowing what I was looking for

or what to call you I think I did not
even know I was looking how would I

have known you when I saw you as I did
time after time when you appeared to me

as you did naked offering yourself
entirely at that moment and you let

me breathe you touch you taste you knowing
no more than I did and only when I

began to think of losing you did I
recognize you when you were already

part memory part distance remaining
mine in the ways that I learn to miss you

from what we cannot hold the stars are made

"From what we cannot hold the stars are made," Merwin concludes. To me, the poem, along with being a love poem, describes the essence of the art of poetry and its burning necessity. Perhaps this is finally the very heart of what poetry can do and be. It gives shape to those empty spaces within us that we have no words for until we find them in a poem.

Poems often begin from a question, or a needling of something disturbing or provoking, sometimes even from ignorance. Robert Frost describes the impulse or sensation for how a poem begins as "a lump in the throat; a sense of wrong, a home-sickness, a loneliness." From there a poet takes elements, either an image, a particular scene or landscape, a memory, maybe only an expression—and appeals to her unconscious, her place of unknowing in hopes that as words, phrases, and fragments take shape, like beads on a string, something original and exciting might evolve. As the poem gestates and comes into being, it gradually becomes clear. It is this mystic negotiation of the knowing and unknowing, that flicker of light in a dark wood that is poetry. And it is through poetry that my own path in the darkness was lit that day when I sat behind my wooden desk in Miss Hudson's fourth grade classroom. Like that lone traveler in the "The Road Not Taken," negotiating between the fork in the yellow road, "knowing how way leads to way," I have never looked back.

# NOTES ON
# CONTRIBUTORS

YEHUDA AMICHAI (1924–2000) was born in Würzburg, Germany, and immigrated to Palestine with his family in 1935. He attended Hebrew University. He published nineteen collections of poetry in English and twelve in Hebrew. He was the recipient of numerous awards, including the Israel Prize in 1982, his country's highest honor. He was nominated several times for the Nobel Prize.

W. H. AUDEN (1907–1973) was born in York, England, and was educated at Christ Church, Oxford. He was awarded the Pulitzer Prize in 1948, the Bollingen Prize in 1953, the National Book Award in 1956, and the National Medal for Literature in 1967.

ELIZABETH BISHOP (1911–1979) was born in Worchester, Massachusetts. She is the author of *Poems: North & South, A Cold Spring, Questions of Travel, The Complete Poems*, and *Geography III*, along with *The Collected Prose* (a compilation of essays and stories). She received the Pulitzer Prize in 1956 and the National Book Award in 1970 for *The Complete Poems*. She was Consultant in Poetry to the Library of Congress from 1949 to 1950.

ROBERT BLY (1926–) was born in western Minnesota and grew up in a community dominated by Norwegian immigrant farmers and their culture. He attended St. Olaf College in Minnesota before transferring to Harvard University. He studied for two years at the University of Iowa Writers' Workshop and traveled on a Fulbright grant to Norway, where he translated Norwegian poetry into English. He is the author of more than thirty books of poetry. *The Light Around the Body* (1967) won the National Book Award. His honors include Guggenheim, Rockefeller, and National Endowment for the Arts fellowships as well as the Robert Frost Medal from the Poetry Society of America.

LOUISE BOGAN (1897–1970) was born in Livermore Falls, Maine. She attended Boston University for a year before leaving to marry. She published six poetry collections and served as the Poetry Consultant to the Library of Congress from 1945 to 1946.

EAVAN BOLAND (1944–) was born in Dublin, Ireland, and was raised in London and New York. She attended Trinity College in Dublin. She has published over twenty poetry collections. Among her many awards and honors are a Jacob's Award, a Lannan Foundation Award in Poetry, and an American Ireland Fund Literary Award.

JOSEPH BRODSKY (1940–1996) was born in Leningrad, Russia. He was exiled from the Soviet Union in 1972 after serving eighteen months in a labor camp. He is most known for *A Part of Speech* (1977) and *To Urania* (1988) and the essay collection *Less Than One* (1986), which won the National Book Critics Circle Award. Brodsky authored fourteen volumes of poetry, as well as several collections of essays. He was awarded the Nobel Prize in Literature in 1987 and was appointed United States Poet Laureate in 1991.

GWENDOLYN BROOKS (1917–2000) was born in Topeka, Kansas, raised in Chicago, Illinois, and educated at Wilson Junior College. She was Poet Laureate of Illinois and served as Consultant in Poetry to the Library of Congress from 1985 to 1986. *Annie Allen* (1949) received the Pulitzer Prize. Among her many awards were more than seventy-five honorary degrees from colleges and universities around the country.

LUCILLE CLIFTON (1936–2010) was born in Buffalo, New York, and studied at Howard University from 1953 to 1955. After that, she studied at the State University of New York at Fredonia. She published thirteen poetry collections and numerous books for children. Her many awards and honors include the Ruth Lilly Poetry Prize, the Juniper Prize from the University of Massachusetts, and the National Book Award. She served as the state of Maryland's Poet Laureate from 1974 until 1985, and she was a Chancellor of the Academy of American Poets.

E. E. CUMMINGS (1894–1962) was born in Cambridge, Massachusetts, and educated at Harvard University. He published over thirty works of poetry. His honors and awards include two Guggenheim fellowships, a Ford Foundation grant, and the Bollingen Prize.

EMILY DICKINSON (1830–1886) was born in Amherst, Massachusetts, and was educated at Mount Holyoke Female Seminary, but left after a year. She wrote nearly eighteen hundred poems.

PAUL LAURENCE DUNBAR (1872–1906) was born in Dayton, Ohio, and did not attend college. He was one of the first African-American poets to gain national recognition. He authored over twenty publications, including poetry collections and works of fiction.

ROBERT FROST (1874–1963) was born in San Francisco, where he lived for eleven years. He attended Dartmouth College and Harvard University but never graduated. In 1912 he moved with his wife and four children to England, where he published his first two books, *A Boy's Will* (1913) and *North of Boston* (1914). He won the Pulitzer Prize four times and served as Consultant in Poetry to the Library of Congress from 1958 to 1959.

LOUISE GLÜCK (1943–) was born in New York City and educated at Sarah Lawrence College and Columbia University. She received the Pulitzer Prize, the National Book Critics Circle Award, and the Bollingen Prize. She is a former Poet Laureate Consultant in Poetry to the Library of Congress (2003–2004).

ROBERT HAYDEN (1913–1980) was born in Detroit, Michigan, attended Detroit City College (renamed Wayne State University), and continued his education at the University of Michigan. He was a Fellow of the American Academy of Poets and Consultant in Poetry to the Library of Congress (1976–1978). He received a Hopwood Award, the Grand Prize for Poetry at the first World Festival of Negro Arts, and the Russell Loines Award from the National Institute of Arts and Letters.

GERARD MANLEY HOPKINS (1844–1889) was born in Stratford, Essex, England, and was educated at Balliol College, Oxford. His works include volumes of poetry, notebooks, papers, sermons, and devotional writings.

LANGSTON HUGHES (1902–1967) was born in Joplin, Missouri, and raised in Kansas and Illinois. He published twenty poetry collections along with over thirty other publications, and he was awarded the Spingarn Medal for distinguished achievements by an African American in 1960 and the National Institute of Arts and Letters in 1961. He received honorary degrees from Lincoln University, Howard University, and Western Reserve University.

DENIS JOHNSON (1949–2017) was born in Munich, West Germany; raised in Tokyo, Manila, and Washington, DC; and educated at the University of Iowa. He published five poetry collections and was the author of numerous novels and short story collections. *Jesus' Son* and *Tree of Smoke* won National Book Awards. He received a Guggenheim Fellowship, the Whiting Award, the Award of Merit Medal in Literature from the American Academy of Arts and Letters, the Arts and Letters Award in Literature, and the Sue Kaufman Prize for First Fiction.

BEN JONSON (1572–1637) was born in London, England, and was educated at the Westminster School. He wrote numerous poems, plays, and masques.

JOHN KEATS (1795–1821) was born in Moorgate, London, and educated at Enfield, a private school. He published three books of poetry: *Lamia, Isabella, The Eve of St. Agnes*, and Other Poems (1820); *Endymion: A Poetic Romance* (1818); and *Poems* (1817).

LI-YOUNG LEE (1957–) was born in Djakarta, Indonesia, to Chinese political exiles. He arrived with his family in the United States in 1964. Lee was a student at the University of Pittsburgh. His many honors include the Lannon Literary Award, and the American Book Award.

ROBERT LOWELL (1917–1977) was born in Boston, Massachusetts, and was educated at Harvard University and Kenyon College. He was appointed the Poet Laureate Consultant in Poetry to the Library of Congress, where he served from 1947 until 1948. In addition to winning the National Book Award, he won the Pulitzer Prize for Poetry in 1947 and 1974, the National Book Critics Circle Award in 1977, and a National Institute of Arts and Letters Award in 1947.

CLAUDE McKAY (1889–1948) was born in Jamaica. He studied at the Tuskegee Institute and at Kansas State College. He published eleven books, which include poetry collections and prose. He was awarded the Musgrave Medal, the Harmon Foundation Award, the James Weldon Johnson Literary Guild Award, and the Order of Jamaica.

W. S. MERWIN (1927–) was born in New York City and raised in Union City, New Jersey, and Scranton, Pennsylvania. He attended Princeton University. His many honors include two Pulitzer Prizes, the National Book Award, and the Tanning Prize. In 2010 he was named the US Poet Laureate.

EDNA ST. VINCENT MILLAY (1892–1950) was born in Rockland, Maine, and was educated at Vassar College. She won the Pulitzer Prize in 1923 for *The Ballad of the Harp-Weaver*. In 1943 she was awarded the Robert Frost Medal for her lifetime contribution to American poetry.

CZESŁAW MIŁOSZ (1911–2004) was born in Lithuania to Polish parents. He graduated from Sigismund Augustus Gymnasium in Vilnius and studied law at Stefan Batory University. He was awarded the Neustadt International Prize for Literature in 1978 and the Nobel Prize for Literature in 1980. In 1999 he was named a Puterbaugh Fellow.

SHARON OLDS (1942–) was born in San Francisco, California and was raised in Berkeley. She attended Stanford University and earned her PhD at Columbia University. Her many honors include the Guggenheim Fellowship, a National Endowment for the Arts Fellowship, the National Book Critics Circle Award, the New York State Poet Laureate, and an Academy of American Poets Fellowship. She is a member of the American Academy of Arts and Sciences. She won the Pulitzer Prize in 2013 for *Stag's Leap*.

SYLVIA PLATH (1932–1963) was born in Boston, Massachusetts. She attended Smith College and earned a Fulbright grant to study at the University of Cambridge in England. Her poetry volumes include *The Colossus*, *Crossing the Water*, *Winter Trees*, *Ariel*, and *The Collected Poems*, which won the Pulitzer Prize.

STANLEY PLUMLY (1939–) was born in Barnesville, Ohio, was educated at Wilmington College, and earned his PhD at Ohio University. His collection *Old Heart* (2009) won the *Los Angeles Times* Book Prize and the Paterson Poetry Prize. His honors and awards include fellowships from the Guggenheim Foundation, the Rockefeller Foundation, the Ingram-Merrill Foundation, and the National Endowment for the Arts. He is a member of the American Academy of Arts and Sciences. Since 2009 he has been Maryland's Poet Laureate.

ADRIENNE RICH (1929–2012) was born in Baltimore, Maryland, and was educated at Radcliffe College. She won the National Book Award for *Diving into the Wreck* (1973) and the National Book Critics Circle Award for *The School Among the Ruins* (2004). Among her other honors are a Guggenheim Fellowship, the Ruth Lilly Poetry Prize, the Bollingen Prize, a MacArthur Fellowship, and the National Book Foundation's Medal for Distinguished Contribution to American Literature. She refused the National Medal of Art in 1997 for political reasons.

RAINER MARIA RILKE (1875–1926) was born in Prague and educated at Charles University (Prague) and the University of Munich. His published volumes of poetry include *Sonnets to Orpheus* and *Divine Elegies*, letters, and a novel.

EDWIN ARLINGTON ROBINSON (1869–1935) was born in Head Tide and raised in Gardiner, Maine, which he renamed "Tilbury Town" in his work. He studied for two years as a special student at Harvard University. He published over thirty collections of poems. *Collected Poems* (1921) was awarded the first Pulitzer Prize for Poetry; he won a second Pulitzer with *The Man Who Died Twice* (1924) and a third with *Tristram* (1927).

THEODORE ROETHKE (1908–1963) was born in Saginaw, Michigan, and was educated at the University of Michigan. He was awarded the Pulitzer Prize for *The Waking* (1954). He also received two Guggenheim Fellowships, the Bollingen Prize, the Shelley Memorial Award, and two National Book Awards.

WILLIAM SHAKESPEARE (1564–1616) was born in Stratford-upon-Avon, England. He received no university education. He wrote over thirty plays and 154 sonnets, as well as a variety of other poems.

GERALD STERN (1925–) was born in Pittsburgh, Pennsylvania, and was educated at the University of Pittsburgh. His volume of poems *Lucky Life* (1977) was the Lamont Poetry Selection of the Academy of American Poets and his book

*This Time: New and Selected Poems* (1998) won the National Book Award. He also received the Wallace Stevens Award and the Library of Congress Rebekah Johnson Bobbitt National Award. He was elected a Chancellor of the Academy of American Poets in 2006.

WALLACE STEVENS (1879–1955) was born in Reading, Pennsylvania, and educated at Harvard University and New York Law School. In 1946 he was elected to the National Institute of Arts and Letters and in 1950 he received the Bollingen Prize in Poetry. He received the National Book Award twice, once for *The Auroras of Autumn* (1950) and once for *The Collected Poems of Wallace Stevens* (1955), which also won the Pulitzer Prize.

ROBERT LOUIS STEVENSON (1850–1894) was born in Edinburgh, Scotland. He attended the University of Edinburgh where he studied law. He published collections of poetry, short stories and thirteen novels.

ANN TAYLOR (1782–1866) was an English poet and literary critic. She is best remembered as the sister of Jane Taylor and collaborator in "The Star." Ann Taylor's poem "The Maniac's Song" was said to be an unacknowledged source for Keat's "La Belle Dame sans Merci."

JANE TAYLOR (1783–1824) was born in London, England. She frequently collaborated with her sister, Ann. She published over eighty poems, one novel, and was a regular contributor to *Youth's Magazine.*

WILLIAM WORDSWORTH (1770–1850) was born in Cockermouth, England, and educated at St. John's College, Cambridge. He wrote more than five hundred sonnets. From 1843 to 1850 he was Poet Laureate of England.

JAMES WRIGHT (1927–1980) was born in Martins Ferry, Ohio. He attended Kenyon College and later continued at the University of Washington. His first volume *The Green Wall* won the Yale Series of Younger Poets Award. He was elected a chancellor of the Academy of American Poets in 1971. His *Collected Poems* (1971) won the Pulitzer Prize.

ADAM ZAGAJEWSKI (1945–) was born in Lvov, Poland. He was awarded the Bronze Cross of Merit and twice received the Officer's Cross of the Order of Polonia Restituta. In 1992 he received a Guggenheim Fellowship. He won the 2004 Neustadt International Prize for Literature, and is the second Polish writer to receive the prize, after Czesław Miłosz. In 2015 he received the Heinrich Mann Prize, and in 2016 the Griffin Poetry Prize Lifetime Recognition Award.

# NOTES

### "We Real Cool"

"Sonia Sanchez writes," *Poetry Speaks Expanded*, Elise Paschen and Rebekah Presson Mosby, editors, Dominique Raccah, series editor, Sourcebooks, Inc., Naperville, Illinois, 2007.

### "The Swing"

Quotation from "The Country Mouse," Elizabeth Bishop, *The Collected Prose*, edited by Robert Giroux, Farrar, Straus and Giroux, New York, 1984.

Robert Louis Stevenson, Shakespeare and *The Arabian Nights* and biographical information, https://www.poets.org/poetsorg/poet/robert-louis-stevenson.

### "I Wandered Lonely as a Cloud"

Dorothy Wordsworth's journal, Wordsworth Trust, wordsworth.org.uk/dorothyjournal.html.

*Preface to Lyrical Ballads* by William Wordsworth, *The Norton Anthology of English Literature*, Vol. 2 revised, H. Abrams, general editor, W. W. Norton & Company, Inc., New York, 1968, 1962.

### "You and Your Whole Race" and "I, Too"

Biographical information, *Poetry Speaks*, pp. 166–68.

"wonderful world of books": "The Uselessness of Tears," Langston Hughes, *Guardian*, Saturday, October 26, 2002, theguardian.com/books/2002/oct/26/featuresreviews.guardianreview37.

Inspiration for "I too": Selected Letters of Langston Hughes, edited by Arnold Rampersad and David Roessel with Christina Fratantoro. Alfred A. Knopf, Random House. New York, 2015, p. 27.

Paul Laurence Dunbar, Carl Sandburg, Claude McKay, and Walt Whitman were his poetic influences, https://www.poets.org/poets org/poet/langston-hughes.

## Psalm 23: "The Lord Is My Shepherd"

Jean Valentine: "The likeness lies in poetry and meditative prayer."

"One Whole Voice" is comprised of extracts from *A God in the House: Poets Talk about Faith,* edited by Ilya Kaminsky and Katherine Towler, Tupelo Press, North Adams, MA, 2012.

Poetry Foundation Website: poetryfoundation.org/poetrymagazine /articles/detail/69770.

## "My child blossoms sadly"

*Paris Review*, Yehuda Amichai, "The Art of Poetry," No. 44, Inter-viewed by Lawrence Joseph, theparisreview.org/interviews/2095 /yehuda-amichai-the-art-of-poetry-no-44-yehuda-amichai.

## "The Snow Man"

*The Necessary Angel: Essays on Reality and the Imagination* by Wallace Stevens, Vintage Books, Alfred A. Knopf, Random House, New York, 1942, p. 4.

Wallace Stevens: "I shall explain," *The Poems of Our Climate,* Harold Bloom, Cornell University Press, Ithaca and London, 1976, p. 63.

## "Stopping by Woods on a Snowy Evening"

*Paris Review,* Robert Frost, "The Art of Poetry," No. 2, interviewed by Richard Poirier, theparisreview.org/interviews/4678/robert-frost -the-art-of-poetry-no-2-robert-frost.

## "Ars Poetica?"

Term "Ars poetica": https://www.poets.org/poetsorg/text/ars-poetica -poetic-term.

"There are some kinds of philosophy," *Paris Review,* Czesław Miłosz, "The Art of Poetry," No. 70, Interviewed by Robert Faggen, www.theparisreview.org/interviews/1721/czeslaw-milosz-the-art -of-poetry-no-70-czeslaw-milosz.

"Emily Dickinson famously said," Thomas Wentworth Higginson, *Atlantic,* October, 1891, Emily Dickinson's Letters, theatlantic.com /past/unbound/poetry/emilyd/edletter.htm.

## "January 1, 1965"

Poem was written when Brodsky was in exile. Poetry Foundation information on poetryfoundation.org/poems-and-poets/poets/detail /joseph-brodsky.

## "Childhood"

Quotation from Rilke's letters: *Letters to a Young Poet*, translation by M. D. Herter Norton, W. W. Norton, New York, 1934, p. 35.

## "I'm Nobody! Who are you?"

Biographical information on Dickinson and quote "had an enormous impact on her verse" from https://www.poets.org/poetsorg /poet/emily-dickinson.

She wrote to Wadsworth after reading a piece he wrote in *The Atlantic Monthly*: *Her Own Society: A new reading of Emily Dickinson*, Judith Thurman, *The New Yorker*, August 4, 2008. https://www .newyorker.com/magazine/2008/08/04/her-own-society.

Brenda Wineapple, *White Heat: The Friendship of Emily Dickinson and Thomas Wentworth Higginson*, Anchor Books, Division of Random House, New York & Canada, 2009, p. 101.

## "'Hope' is the Thing With Feathers"

Emily Dickinson Letters to Thomas Wentworth Higginson, *Atlantic*, October 1891, theatlantic.com/past/unbound/poetry/emilyd/edletter .htm.

## "My Papa's Waltz"

Theodore Roethke: "men can experience other people's experience," youtube.com/watch?v=aV8h3WqjN9c. McGraw-Hill Films, *In a Dark Time: A Film About Theodore Roethke*, by David Myers, sponsored by the Poetry Center.

### "Poppies in October"

*Last Looks, Last Books: Stevens, Plath, Lowell, Bishop, Merrill*, by Helen Vendler, Princeton University Press, 2010, Board of Trustees, National Gallery of Art, p. 68.

### "Confession"

Interview with Louise Glück was conducted by Grace Cavalieri for the radio series, "The Poet and the Poem from the Library of Congress," during the Library's bicentennial celebration in 2000.

### "The Sisters of Sexual Treasure"

"Advice to Young Poets: Sharon Olds in Conversation with Michael Lasky," Poets.org, Academy of American Poets, poets.org/poetsorg /text/advice-young-poets-sharon-olds-conversation.

### "Sympathy"

Biographical material about Dunbar, parents as freed slaves, education and employment, *The Norton Anthology of African American Literature*. Henry Louis Gates, Jr. and Nellie Y. McKay, General Editors. W. W. Norton & Company, New York, 2004, p. 905.

And Academy of American Poets, https://www.poets.org/poetsorg/poet /paul-laurence-dunbar.

### "Bright Star"

John Keats: "The principle of beauty," *Selected letters of John Keats*, Revised Edition, Edited by Grant F. Scott, Harvard University Press, Cambridge, MA, 2005, p. 272.

### "A Blessing"

*Paris Review*, James Wright, "The Art of Poetry," No. 19, Interviewed by Peter Stitt. theparisreview.org/interviews/3839/james-wright -the-art-of-poetry-no-19-james-wright.

### "My Mother's Feet"

About Stanley Plumly's father, Academy of American Poets, poets. org/poetsorg/poet/stanley-plumly from interview, *Iowa Review*, Vol. 4 no. 4, Fall, 1973.

### "Taking the Hands"

Robert Bly: "interested in the connection." poetryfoundation.org/poems
-and-poets/poets/detail/robert-bly.

Deep image poetic term: From Poetry Foundation Glossary of poetic
terms: https://www.poetryfoundation.org/learn/glossary-terms/deep
-image.

### "What lips my lips have kissed, and where, and why"

Her biographer Nancy Milford: *Savage Beauty: The Life of Edna St.
Vincent Millay*, Random House, New York, 2001, p. xxii.

### "fury"

On Lucille Clifton: *The Prentice Hall Anthology of Women's Literature*,
Deborah H. Holdstein, Pearson Education: Upper Saddle River,
NJ, 2000, p. 737.

### "Diving into the Wreck"

Eavan Boland quote: *Lives of the Poets* by Michael Schmidt, Vintage
Books, Division of Random House, New York, 2010, p. 856.

### "Song for the Last Act"

Richard Howard quotation from *Poetry Speaks*, p. 150.

Marianne Moore quotation: "compactness compacted." *Poems and
New Poems*, revised edition by Louise Bogan. *Nation*, Nov. 15,
1941, p. 486.

### "Musée des Beaux Arts"

*Paris Review,* W. H. Auden, "The Art of Poetry," No. 17.

Interviewed by Michael Newman. theparisreview.org/interviews/3970
/w-h-auden-the-art-of-poetry-no-17w-h-auden.

### "One Art"

*On Elizabeth Bishop*, Colm Toíbín, Princeton University Press, Prince-
ton and Oxford, 2015, p. 4.

### "Waking in the Blue"

Robert Lowell: "Confessional Verse," Michael Schmidt, *The Lives of
the Poets*, p. 814.

Robert Lowell: "A poetry of symptoms," Michael Schmidt, *The Lives of the Poets*, p. 815.

Robert Lowell: "Lithium treatment," *The Letters of Robert Lowell*, edited by Saskia Hamilton, Farrar, Straus and Giroux, New York, 2005, introduction, p. xvii.

Letter to Berryman: *The Letters of Robert Lowell*, p. 352.

### "The Pomegranate"

Eavan Boland: "Motherhood was central," Smartish Pace, A Poetry Review, Q&A with Eavan Boland, smartishpace.com/pqa/eavan _boland/.

### "Nick and the Candlestick"

Plath: "she said of her poetics," "A 1962 Sylvia Plath Interview with Peter Orr," *Modern American Poetry*, english.illinois.edu/MAPS /POETS/M_R/PLATH/orrinterview.htm.

Plath: Placing her husband's first book, Keith Sager, "Hughes, Edward James (1930–1988)" *Oxford Dictionary of National Biography*. Oxford University Press, 2004.

Plath seeks to universalize her experience to, in effect, "render impersonal the (apparently) intense personal," Michael Schmidt, *Lives of the Poets*, p. 829–830.

### "Try to Praise the Mutilated World"

"Zagajewski writes," "Adam Zagajewski: The Poet of 9/11," by Matthew Kaminski, *Newsweek*, newsweek.com/adam-zagajewski -poet-911-67385.

### "The Child Is Father to the Man"

William Wordsworth: Michael Schmidt, *Lives of the Poets*, p. 499

### "Teachers"

W. S. Merwin: "Writing poetry always has," PBS interview with Bill Moyers, pbs.org/moyers/journal/06262009/transcript1.html.

"The Shadow of Sirius," PBS interview with Bill Moyers.

Robert Frost: "a lump in the throat," poetryfoundation.org/poems -and-poets/poets/detail/robert-frost.

# PERMISSIONS

# ACKNOWLEDGMENTS

This book would not be possible without the encouragement and sensitivity of Peter Borland, my brilliant editor. It began with a conversation about the poems that were crucial to my coming of age and miraculously blossomed into this surprising memoir. Huge gratitude to my friends at Atria: Daniella Wexler, Lisa Sciambra, Hillary Tisman, and Judith Curr. Special gratitude to Nancy Palmquist for her friendship, generosity, and discerning eye. I have benefitted tremendously from the insight, brilliance, and implicit trust of my agent Sarah Chalfant, thank you, and special thanks to the remarkable Jacqueline Ko and Jin Auh at the Wylie Agency. My family, Lucas and David, no words can describe my gratitude for your sustaining presence in my life, for understanding my need to put words to paper and for indulging my occasional desire to read poems to you aloud. Finally, I'm grateful to all the poets living and deceased whose work has enriched my life. I hesitate to imagine who I would be without your words.